Mark Illustrated in Latin

Mark Illustrated in Latin

Fredrick J. Long

GlossaHouse
Wilmore, KY
www.GlossaHouse.com

Mark Illustrated in Latin
Copyright © 2018 by GlossaHouse

All rights reserved. No part of this work may be reproduced or transmitted in any form or by any means, electronic or mechani-cal, including photocopying and recording, or by means of any information storage or retrieval system, except as may be ex-pressly permitted by the 1976 Copyright Act or in writing from the publisher. Requests for permission should be addressed in writing to the following:

GlossaHouse, LLC
110 Callis Circle
Wilmore, KY 40390

Bible. Mark. Latin, Clementine Vulgate, 1598.
 Mark Illustrated in Latin / Fredrick J. Long.
– Wilmore, KY : GlossaHouse, [© 2018].

> 70 pages : color illustrations ; 28 cm. – (GlossaHouse Illustrated Biblical Texts. Latin-English Bible. Bible)

> Summary: The Latin text of the Gospel of Mark is set within colorful illustrations to represent narration, dialogue, monologue, and scripture quotations, together with an English Translation. Text in English and Latin.

> ISBN: 978-1942697527 (paperback)

> Library of Congress Control Number: 2018911428

> 1. Bible. Mark – Cartoons and comics.   I. Long, Fredrick J., 1966- III. Title. IV. Series. V. Latin (Clementine Vulgate). 1598. VI. Bible. Mark. English. 2018.

The Clementine Vulgate is in the public domain and was obtained and used with permission from The Clementine Text Project at http://vulsearch.sourceforge.net/index.html.

The English translation of the Clementine Vulgate of Mark has been created by Fredrick J. Long copyright © 2018.

The fonts used to create this work are available from linguistsoftware.com/lgku.htm. Illustrations and general illustration layout Copyright © 2006 Neely Publishing LLC.

Cover Design by T. Michael W. Halcomb
Book Design by T. Michael W. Halcomb
Updated Layout by Fredrick J. Long
Illustration Design by Keith Neely

GlossaHouse Illustrated Biblical Texts

SERIES EDITORS

T. Michael W. Halcomb
Fredrick J. Long
Timothy McNinch

LAETA
Latin: Ancient Education Tools & Aids

SERIES EDITOR

T. Michael W. Halcomb

VOLUME EDITOR

Fredrick J. Long

LAETA

The Latin term LAETA is an adjective that means "fertile" or "welcoming," especially when describing land. It is also a term that captures the link between this series and its Hebrew (HA'ARETS) and Greek (AGROS) counterparts also bearing land-related names and published by GlossaHouse. In keeping with those series, LAETA functions as an acronym: Latin: Ancient Educational Tools & Aids. This series exists because, while there are many great resources on Latin, more can and always will need to be created. Thus, LAETA welcomes new and innovative works, those that make a contribution, however big or small, to the journey of learning Latin. The long-term aim is to create a tiered curriculum suite featuring innovative readers, grammars, specialized studies, and similar resources that will both encourage and foster the use of Latin. Additionally, the LAETA series endeavors to facilitate the creation and publication of innovative and inexpensive print and digital resources within the context of the global community.

Table of Contents

Introduction   x-xv

Evangelium secundum Marcum (GOSPEL ACCORDING TO MARK)

Caput I (Ch. 1)	1-5
Caput II (Ch. 2)	5-9
Caput III (Ch. 3)	9-13
Caput IV (Ch. 4)	13-17
Caput V (Ch. 5)	17-21
Caput VI (Ch. 6)	21-28
Caput VII (Ch. 7)	28-32
Caput VIII (Ch. 8)	32-35
Caput IX (Ch. 9)	35-40
Caput X (Ch. 10)	40-45
Caput XI (Ch. 11)	45-49
Caput XII (Ch. 12)	49-53
Caput XIII (Ch. 13)	53-55
Caput XIV (Ch. 14)	56-63
Caput XV (Ch. 15)	63-68
Caput XVI (Ch. 16)	68-70

INTRODUCTION TO *ILLUSTRATED MARK IN LATIN*

In this volume, I am pleased to offer the most recent edition to the GlossaHouse Illustrated Biblical Texts. Let me explain about its illustrations, the Latin base text, versification differences from standard Greek and English versions, and aspects of the English translation of the Latin.

I. ILLUSTRATIONS: The GlossaHouse Illustrated Biblical Texts feature the illustrations of Keith Neely. In this volume, the Latin text of Mark comes to life with Neely's beautiful and colorful illustrations that include narrative text boxes and speech text bubbles. Great care was taken to best place these boxes and bubbles so as not to obscure the illustrations, but to help bring them to life. Prominence is given to the speech bubbles by having them, if overlapping, placed slightly on top of the narrative introductions in the text boxes.

II. LATIN BASE TEXT: The Latin edition used is that of Clementine from 1592 (3rd edition, 1598) under the title *Biblia Sacra Vulgatae Editionis Sixti Quinti Pont. Max. iussu recognita atque edita* (Typographia Apostolica Vaticana). It is named after Pope Clement VIII who called for its creation. In textual critical editions of the NT, such as the Nestle-Aland^{28} and the UBS^5, the Clementine Vulgate is indicated by vg^{cl}.[1] The Clementine text was the official version of the Vulgate until 1979, then replaced by the Neo-Vulgate edition. The value of the Clementine Vulgate is that it represents a Latin edition that is close to the Byzantine Greek tradition, or what was edited into the Majority Text. The Clementine Latin spellings contain some idiosyncrasies, most notable the use of a "j" instead of an "i" in the pronoun *eius*—thus one finds *ejus* in the Clementine Vulgate. We have not changed these idiosyncrasies.

In this volume, we are using the most recent Clementine edition that is in the public domain and found at The Clementine Text Project at http://vulsearch.sourceforge.net/html/Mt.html. It is used with permission. Important features of this project taken from this website are given in A.–C. immediately below (slightly edited).

  A. About the project—The Clementine Text Project was an effort between 2002 and 2005 to create a free online text version of the Clementine Vulgate. This is an historically important edition of the Latin Bible that previously did not exist in electronic form. Many people generously gave their time to help create and proof-read the new text. Work to maintain the text and correct errors that are found is ongoing: the latest update was on Jan 23 2018.

  B. The version of the text—There is a single, definitive Clementine text, namely the Editio Typica published by the Typographus Vaticanus in 1598 under the title *Biblia Sacra Vulgatæ editionis, Sixti V Pontificis Maximi jussu recognita et edita*. However, the text here has necessarily been derived from later sources, principally that edited by A. Colunga and L. Turrado (La Editorial

---

[1] Eberhard Nestle, et al. *Novum Testamentum Graece*, 28th rev. ed. (Stuttgart: Deutsche Bibelstiftung, 2012) and Kurt Aland, et al. *Greek New Testament*, 5th rev. ed. (Stuttgart: Deutsche Bibelstiftung, 2014), 26.

Católica, Madrid, 1946). For dubious readings, the editions of C. Vercellone (Typis S. Congregationis de Propaganda Fide, Rome, 1861) and M. Hetzenauer (Pustet & Co., 1914) were also consulted. Only the canonical books are included (many printed versions include an appendix with the apocryphal books Oratio Manassæ and Esdræ III and IV).

C. **Editorial decisions**—The words of the text have been transcribed as accurately as possible, human error notwithstanding. The usual division into books, chapters, and verses is observed. Punctuation, which varies widely between different editions, has been chosen with readability in mind; the text is divided into paragraphs for the same purpose. In the poetry sections, the text is presented split into lines, following Colunga and Turrado, who themselves in their Præfatio say they follow other 'recentiores editiones' in this.

Where there are minor variations in spelling amongst the previous editions, the new version generally adopts those spellings most familiar from the liturgical books printed in the first half of the twentieth century. It also distinguishes the semivowel j, and represents the diphthongs ae and oe by ligatures (æ and œ). Examples of the latter are seen in Mark 1:14–15—*Postquam autem traditus est Joannes, venit Jesus in Galilæam, prædicans Evangelium regni Dei,* 15 *et dicens: Quoniam Impletum est tempus, et appropinquavit regnum Dei: pœnitemini, et credite Evangelio.*

III. **VERSIFICATION AND OTHER DIFFERENCES FROM GREEK AND ENGLISH VERSIONS**: In a number of places, the Clementine Vulgate shows interesting variations from versions that you may be more familiar with. Below are some of the most notable ones:

- Greek Texts have 4:41, but the Clementine Vulgate includes the content of this verse in 4:40.
- The Greek text of 6:9 has Jesus suddenly speaking in direct discourse after indirect commands, "And don't ["you" plural] wear two tunics!" (καὶ μὴ ἐνδύσησθε δύο χιτῶνας) whereas the Latin continues recording Jesus's indirect commands as "and [that they] not be clothed with two coats" (*et ne induerentur duabus tunicis*). The Greek tradition shows a minor variant here with infinitives (ενδυσασθαι or ενδεδυσθαι).
- The Latin records indirect question in 8:23—"he asked him if he saw anything" (*interrogavit eum si quid videret*)—whereas the best Greek witnesses have a direct question "do you see something?"
- The Latin contains an extra command at the end of 8:26—"And if you enter the village, speak to no one" (*et si in vicum introieris, nemini dixeris*).
- The Versification of Mark 9 is quite different from the Greek text, since 8:39 in the Latin is 9:1 in the Greek. Thus, 9:1 in the Latin is 9:2 in the Greek.
- In 10:49a the Latin has an indirect command, "And standing, Jesus ordered him to be summoned" (*Et stans Jesus præcepit illum vocari*) whereas the Greek has direct speech 10:49a "And standing, Jesus said, 'Summon him.'" (καὶ στὰς ὁ Ἰησοῦς εἶπεν, Φωνήσατε αὐτόν).
- In 11:32 the religious authorities in the Latin text admit they would have reason to fear the people if they answered of John the Baptist that his baptism was "from humans" whereas in the Greek/English this is a narrative comment. So, in Latin, "If we say, 'From humans,' we

fear the people" (*Si dixerimus: Ex hominibus, timemus populum.* [I have added a period here]) but in Greek it is punctuated as a question and reads, "Should we say, 'From humans'?—they were fearing the people." The Latin appears to smooth out the Greek which is a bit rough.

- In 12:28b, the Latin has an indirect question "they were asking him what was the first commandment of all" (*interrogavit eum quod esset primum omnium mandatum*) whereas the Greek has a direct question, "What is the first commandment of all?"

IV. **ENGLISH BASE TRANSLATION AT THE BOTTOM OF THE PAGE**: In order to help students or translators with obscure words or wording, a fresh English translation and placed at the bottom of the page. This translation has started with the Douay-Rheims Bible (revised by Richard Challoner) but significantly altered to be its own translation. Let me explain a bit about my translation philosophy.

A. **Latin word order** is preserved as long as this still makes "good" English sense, especially when some sort of prominence attended the fronted word order.

B. **Implied words**, most often objects of verbs such as *it, him, them,* are often included inside parentheses to help convey good English sense. The addition of such words was kept at a minimum; to place them inside parentheses may reveals to readers where the Latin text may co-relate verbs by sharing the same objects, which may contribute to understanding the tone or atmosphere of the event or its description.

C. **Gender inclusiveness** is preserved as much as possible. Thus, the phrase "Son of Man" in reference to Jesus is translated as "Son of Humanity." In most places the noun *homo, hominis* "a human being, man"[2] is translated "person" rather than "man."

D. **Punctuation** decisions are difficult. For imperatives and statements involving feeling, exclamation marks were used to help capture that tone and feeling. Thus, for example, I added capitalization and exclamation marks to the Latin of 11:9–10—*Hosanna! Benedictus qui venit in nomine Domini! Benedictum quod venit regnum patris nostri David! Hosanna in excelsis!* This punctuation then is reflected in my corresponding English translation.

Also, I attempted to follow the punctuation conventions of the Vulgate text; however, most colons (:) were translated as semi-colons (;), unless introducing direct speech where I then used a comma (,). Also, occasionally commas (,) in the Latin text may not have been replicated in translation because this would have made the discourse seem rather "choppy."

E. **Every particle, conjunction,** and **adverb** has been translated as much as possible, including the very frequently occurring instances of *et* and to a much lesser extent *autem* and *enim*.

F. The **Latin relative pronoun (*Qui*)** in a number of places translates the Greek construction of definite article + participle. Thus, for example, the Greek has the following for 10:22:

---

[2] Charlton T. Lewis and Charles Short, *Harpers' Latin Dictionary* (New York: Harper & Brothers, 1891), 860.

22 ὁ δὲ στυγνάσας ἐπὶ τῷ λόγῳ ἀπῆλθεν λυπούμενος· ἦν γὰρ ἔχων κτήματα πολλά.
22 But he, being shocked at the word, departed grieving; for he was having many possessions.

Here the article is translated "he" since it is in a construction of alternating between subjects in conversation. Compare this with the Latin and Translation below in context in which the relative pronoun *Qui* is used in place of the article. Sometimes, when it is clear who the "who" is, I have translated the relative pronoun as such to reflect this interesting construction.

20 At ille respondens, ait illi: Magister, hæc omnia observavi a juventute mea.
21 Jesus autem intuitus eum, dilexit eum, et dixit ei: Unum tibi deest: vade, quæcumque habes vende, et da pauperibus, et habebis thesaurum in cælo: et veni, sequere me.
22 <u>Qui</u> contristatus in verbo, abiit mœrens: erat enim habens multas possessiones.

20 But he, answering back, said to him, "Master, all these things I have observed from my youth."
21 However, Jesus, looking at him, loved him and said to him, "One thing is lacking for you. Go, sell whatsoever you have and give to the poor, and you shall have treasure in heaven; and come, follow me."
22 <u>Who</u>, being struck sad at the saying, went away mourning; for he was having many possessions.

G. **Verb tenses in the indicative mood** are translated somewhat consistently.

- The <u>present tense</u> was preserved in translation even in historical narrative; for example, in Mark 5:9b, "And he <u>says</u> to him: 'My name is Legion, for we are many.'" (*Et <u>dicit</u> ei: Legio mihi nomen est, quia multi sumus*). These present tense verb forms may be considered the equivalent to what is called the Historic Present in Greek. The purpose of the Historical Present is debated; Do they make the narrative more vivid? Most likely, these historic presents serve to highlight events that are forthcoming prominent (not necessarily the direct action of the verb itself).[3]

    In the Latin of Mark's Gospel, we commonly find the present tense Latin *dicit* which translates the Greek present tense verb form λέγει "he says" (1:44; 2:8; 3:4, etc.; although not at 3:9; 8:29; 13:36). More interesting is the Latin *ait* that may be parsed as either present or perfect tense. It occurs seventy-eight times and in a majority of instances (forty-seven), this translates the historic present Greek form λέγει (1:38, 41; 2:5, 10, 14, 17, etc.). However, there are thirty-one instances when this is not true when it translates the underlying Greek aorist εἶπεν "he said" (2:19; 4:40; 6:22, 37; 7:29; 9:20, 22, 35; 10:5, 14, 38, 39, 52; 11:29; 12:15, 32, 43; 13:2; 14:18, 20, 22, 48; 15:39) or the underlying Greek aorist ἔφη "he said" (9:11; 10:20, 29; 12:24; 14:29). In three instances (6:16; 8:24; 15:12) the Latin *ait* translates the underlying Greek imperfect ἔλεγεν "he was saying." To help

---

[3] See a summary of the debate and issues in Fredrick J. Long, *Koine Greek Grammar: A Beginning-Intermediate Exegetical and Pragmatic Handbook* (Wilmore, KY: GlossaHouse, 2015), 125–27, 245–47.

students understand the dual parsing of the Latin *ait*, I will translate it as present tense when there is an underlying present tense in Greek and as a perfect when the underlying Greek is aorist or imperfect.

- <u>Imperfect indicative verb forms</u> were often translated as progressive pasts as in, for example, "He was teaching" (*docebat*). This was for the sake of preserving the imperfective aspect of tense and to alert students to the underlying imperfect. Mark uses several verbs to indicate "amazement," which are not infrequently used in the imperfect tense. However, with verbs of emotional response, a past progressive translation was difficult to arrive at since English verbs of emotional response or fear do not convey past progressive action. Consider the difference between "They were amazed-astonished" and "They were being amazed-astonished."
- The <u>perfect tense</u> was often translated as a simple past ("he taught") and the <u>pluperfect</u> as perfect past ("he had taught").

H. **"Recitative"** *Quia* **and Quoniam "that"** which introduce direct quotations are found in the Vulgate. This capitalized *Quia* or *Quoniam* that comes after a colon actually functions to introduce the following direct quotation. This discourse feature is akin to the Greek use of ὅτι "that" (called recitative ὅτι), for which I will provide further comments in the next paragraph below. So, for example, Mark 2:12b has in Latin: … *ita ut mirarentur omnes, et honorificent Deum, dicentes: <u>Quia</u> numquam sic vidimus* "… so that all wondered and glorified God, saying <u>this</u>: 'We never saw the like!'" Notice that the *Quia* is here translated "this" which will be the practice in my English translation. In the speech bubble, I will capitalize the actual beginning of the quotation, so above will be changed to … *dicentes: Quia <u>Numquam</u>*….[4] This feature with *Quia* or *Quoniam* occurs in 1:15, 37; 2:12; 3:21, 22 (twice); 5:23, 28, 35; 6:4, 14, 15 (twice), 23; 7:20 (with a comma, no colon); 8:16 (lower case *quia*); 9:25, 30; 10:33 (after a period); 11:17; 12:6, 29; 13:6 (no colon and lower case *quia*); 14:58 (first instance), 69, 71, but not at 8:2, 14:27, and 16:14 where the meaning of *quia* (lower case) is "because." In each of these instances, the *Quia* translates the underlying recitative ὅτι in the Greek text. Why were the Greek ὅτι and the Latin *Quia* used to introduce direct quotations? First, *Quia* isn't often used to introduce direct quotations, and there are important verses where it is not used when one might possibly expect one (15:39). Second, there are instances where the underlying Greek uses a recitative ὅτι and the Latin does not use *Quia* or *Quoniam*—1:40; 2:17 (but the ὅτι is missing in some manuscripts); 3:11; 6:18, 35; 7:6 (but the ὅτι is missing in some manuscripts); 8:4, 28 (but the ὅτι is missing in some manuscripts); 12:7; 14:27, 58 (second instance), and 72.

Many grammar books say not to translate ὅτι "that" when introducing direct speech, but I disagree and always do with "this" as an offsetting and forward pointing device. In Greek translation, when the ὅτι is used to introduce direct discourse, it works very well to translate it as "…. *this*: …." to begin the quotation. For example (just making this up): "Jesus answered back and said to them this: 'Do not be afraid!'" For a further discussion of recitative ὅτι, see my *Koine Greek Grammar* in which I say this:

---

[4] Note that in 10:33 it was necessary to place the *Quia* at the end of v.32.

b. *Recitative ὅτι: Semantics and Pragmatics.* Levinsohn (ch.16) has been interested in describing the discourse pragmatic function of ὅτι in narrative with verbs of saying. His conclusions are that in John and Luke-Acts such explicit use of ὅτι occurs at the culmination of a unit or sub-unit, i.e., the ὅτι will "signal that the quotation it introduces culminates an argument" (269). He also notes that in Luke's and John's Gospel the statement Ἀμὴν ἀμὴν λέγω ὑμῖν/σοι *truly, truly I say to you*, when followed by ὅτι, is used to explicate previous teaching.[5][1] From a semantic and marked prominence perspective, I would maintain that recitative ὅτι is a more marked construction than not having ὅτι; thus fittingly and pragmatically, ὅτι may be used to highlight previous teaching or direct quotation that would culminate argumentation or (sub-)units. However, these pragmatic, contextual functions are not inherent to the semantics of the construction. *Rather, it is simply enough to say that recitative ὅτι is marked +prominence for introducing direct speech.* I would tentatively suggest a translation of *this:* prior to the start of the speech quotation, since *this:* sets off and anticipates what follows formally in English. For example, Mark 3:11–12 occurs near the end of a unit (which ends formally in 3:12; NASB95; ESV, NIV, etc.) in a generalizing statement.

Mark 3:11-12 καὶ τὰ πνεύματα τὰ ἀκάθαρτα, ὅταν αὐτὸν ἐθεώρουν, προσ-έπιπτον αὐτῷ καὶ ἔκραζον λέγοντα <u>ὅτι</u> Σὺ εἶ ὁ υἱὸς τοῦ θεοῦ. ¹² καὶ πολλὰ ἐπετίμα αὐτοῖς ἵνα μὴ αὐτὸν φανερὸν ποιήσωσιν.
¹¹ And the unclean spirits, whenever they were seeing him, were falling down before him and were crying out saying <u>this:</u> "You yourself are the Son of God!" ¹² And many times he was rebuking them, in order that they would not make him known.[6]

—Fredrick J. Long, October 2018

---

[5] See also Stephen H. Levinsohn, "Ὅτι Recitativum in John's Gospel: A Stylistic or a Pragmatic Device?," *Work Papers of the Summer Institute of Linguistics, University of North Dakota Session* 43 (1999): 1-14. Online: http://www.und.edu/dept/linguistics/wp/1999Levinsohn.PDF.

[6] Long, *Koine Greek Grammar*, 158–59.

Evangelium secundum Marcum

1:1 The beginning of the gospel of Jesus Christ, the Son of God. 2 As it is written in Isaiah the prophet, "Behold I send my messenger before your face, who will prepare the way before you. 3 A voice of one crying in the desert, 'Prepare the way of the Lord; make straight his paths.'" 4 John was in the desert, baptizing and preaching the baptism of repentance in the remission of sins. 5 And there was going out to him all the country of Judea and all Jerusalemites and they were being baptized by him in the river of Jordan, confessing their sins. 6 And John was clothed with camel's hair and with a leathern girdle about his loins, and he was eating locusts and wild honey. 7 And he was preaching, saying, "There comes after me one mightier than I, the latchet of whose shoes I am not worthy to stoop down and loose. 8 I have baptized you with water; but he will baptize you with the Holy Spirit."

Mark 1:9-20

9 And it came to pass, in those days Jesus came from Nazareth of Galilee and was baptized by John in the Jordan. 10 And immediately coming up out of the water, he saw the heavens open and the Spirit as a dove descending and remaining on him. 11 And there came a voice from heaven: "You are my beloved Son; in you I am well pleased!" 12 And immediately the Spirit drove him out into the desert. 13 And he was in the desert forty days and forty nights, and was tempted by Satan. And he was with beasts; and the angels were ministering to him. 14 And after John was delivered up, Jesus came to Galilee, preaching the gospel of the kingdom of God, 15 And saying this: "The time is accomplished and the kingdom of God is at hand. Repent and believe the gospel!" 16 And passing by the sea of Galilee, he saw Simon and Andrew his brother, casting nets into the sea (for they were fishermen). 17 And Jesus said to them, "Come after me; and I will make you to become fishers of men." 18 And immediately leaving their nets, they followed him. 19 And going on from there a little farther, he saw James the son of Zebedee and John his brother, who also were mending their nets in the ship; 20 and immediately he called them. And leaving their father Zebedee in the ship with his hired hands, they followed him.

Mark 1:21-28

21 And they entered into Capernaum; and immediately on the Sabbath days going into the synagogue, he was teaching them. 22 And they were astonished at his teaching. For he was teaching them as one having power, and not as the scribes. 23 And there was in their synagogue a person with an unclean spirit; and he cried out, 24 saying, "What have we to do with you, Jesus of Nazareth? Have you come to destroy us? I know who you are, the Holy One of God!" 25 And Jesus threatened him, saying, "Speak no more, and go out of the person." 26 And the unclean spirit, tearing him and crying out with a loud voice, went out of him. 27 And they were all amazed so that they thus questioned among themselves, saying, "What thing is this? What is this new teaching? For with power he commands even the unclean spirits, and they obey him." 28 And the fame of him was spread immediately into all the country of Galilee.

Mark 1:29-37

29 And immediately going out of the synagogue they came into the house of Simon and Andrew, with James and John. 30 And Simon's wife's mother was laying down burning up with fever; and immediately they tell him of her. 31 And coming to her, he lifted her up taking her by the hand; and immediately the fever left her, and she was ministering to them. 32 And when evening came after the sun set, they were bringing to him all doing poorly and that were possessed with demons. 33 And all the city was gathered together at the door. 34 And he healed many that were troubled with various diseases. And he cast out many demons; and he was not permitting them to speak, because they were knowing him. 35 And arising very early in the morning, going out he departed into a deserted place, and there he was praying. 36 And Simon pursued after him and the ones who were with him. 37 And when they had found him, they said to him this, "All are seeking for you."

Mark 1:38-2:2

38 And he says to them, "Let us go into the neighboring towns and cities, so that I may preach there also; for I came for this." 39 And he was preaching in their synagogues and in all Galilee and casting out demons. 40 And there came a leper to him, beseeching him and kneeling down, said to him, "If you want you can make me clean." 41 And Jesus, having compassion on him, stretched forth his hand and touching him says to him, "I want. Be made clean!" 42 And when he had spoken, immediately the leprosy departed from him, and he was made clean. 43 And he strictly charged him and immediately sent him away, 44 and he says to him, "See [that] you tell no one; but go, show yourself to the high priest and offer for your cleansing which things Moses commanded for a testimony to them." 45 But he, going out, began to proclaim and to spread the word, so that thus now he could not openly go into the city, but was out of doors in desert places. And they were flocking to him from everywhere. 2:1 And again he entered into Capernaum after (some) days. 2 And it was heard that he was in the house. And many came together, so that there was no room not even at the door. And he was speaking to them the word.

Mark 2:3-11

3 And they came to him bringing a paralytic man, who was carried by four. 4 And when they were not able offer him to him because of the multitude, they uncovered the roof where he was; and opening it, they let down the bed on which the paralytic man was lying. 5 And when Jesus had seen their faith, he says to the paralytic man, "Son, your sins are forgiven you." 6 And there were some of the scribes sitting there and thinking in their hearts, 7 "Why does this one speak in this way? He blasphemes. Who can forgive sins, but God alone?" 8 Which Jesus immediately knowing in his spirit that they so thought within themselves, says to them, "Why do you think these things in your hearts? 9 Which is easier, to say to the paralytic man, 'Your sins are forgiven you'; or to say, 'Arise, take up your bed and walk'? 10 But that you may know that the Son of Humanity has power on earth to forgive sins (he says to the paralytic man), 11 'To you I say, Arise! Take up your bed and go into your house.'"

Mark 2:12-16

12 And immediately he arose and, taking up his bed, went his way in the sight of all, so that all were amazed and were glorifying God, saying this: "We never saw the like!" 13 And he went forth again to the sea side; and all the multitude was coming to him. And he was teaching them. 14 And when he was passing by, he saw Levi, the son of Alpheus, sitting at the toll booth, and he says to him, "Follow me!" And rising up, he followed him. 15 And it came to pass when he was reclining in his house, many tax collectors and sinners were sitting down together with Jesus and his disciples. For there were many who were also following him. 16 And the scribes and the Pharisees, seeing that he was eating with tax collectors and sinners, were saying to his disciples, "Why does your master eat and drink with tax collectors and sinners?"

Mark 2:17-22

17 Jesus hearing this, says to them, "The healthy have no need of a physician, but they that are doing poorly. For I came not to call the just, but sinners." 18 And there were disciples of John and the Pharisees fasting. And they come and say to him, "Why do the disciples of John and of the Pharisees fast, but your disciples do not fast?" 19 And Jesus said to them, "Are the sons of the marriage able to fast, as long as the bridegroom is with them? As long as they have the bridegroom with them, they are not able to fast. 20 But the days will come when the bridegroom will be taken away from them; and then they will fast in those days. 21 No one sews a piece of raw cloth to an old garment; otherwise, the new piece pulls away from the old, and there is made a greater tear. 22 And no one puts new wine into old wineskins; otherwise, the wine will burst the skins, and both the wine will be spilled and the skins will be lost. But new wine must be put into new skins."

Mark 2:23-3:4

23 And it happened again (that) the Lord was walking through the corn fields on the Sabbath, and his disciples began to go forward and to pluck the (heads of) grain. 24 And the Pharisees were saying to him, "Behold, why do they do on the Sabbath what is not lawful?" 25 And he said to them, "Have you never read what David did when he had need, and was hungry himself, and those who were with him? 26 How he entered into the house of God, under Abiathar the high priest, and ate the loaves of presentation, which was not lawful to eat except for the priests, and gave to those who were with him?" 27 And he was saying to them, "The Sabbath was made for humanity, and not humanity for the Sabbath." 28 Therefore the Son of Humanity is Lord, also of the Sabbath. 3:1 And he entered again into the synagogue; and there was a person there who had a withered hand. 2 And they were watching him whether he would heal on the Sabbath days, so that they might accuse him. 3 And he said to the person who had the withered hand, "Stand up in the middle." 4 And he says to them, "Is it lawful to do good on the Sabbath days, or to do evil? To save life, or to destroy?" But they were remaining silent.

Mark 3:5-12

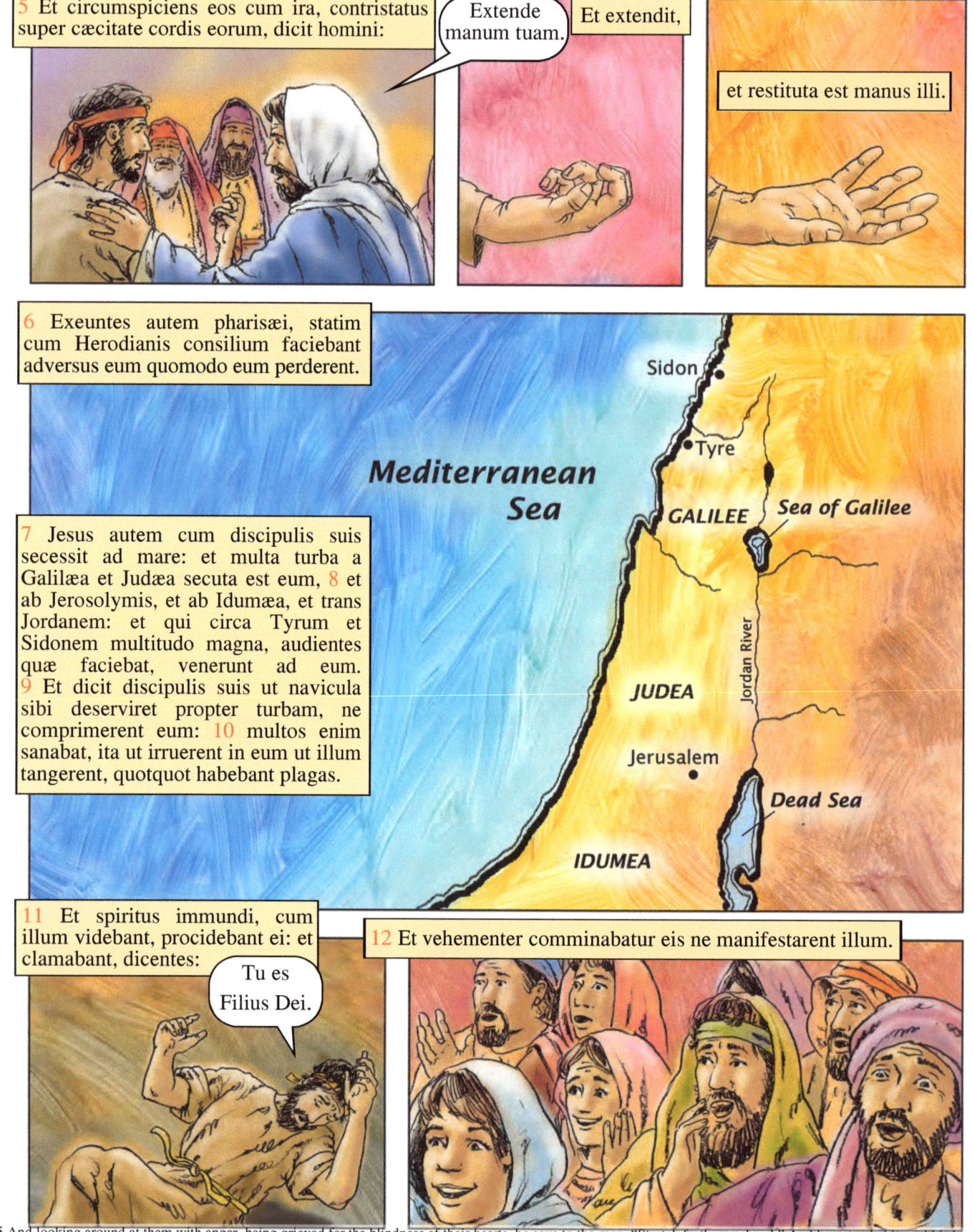

5 Et circumspiciens eos cum ira, contristatus super cæcitate cordis eorum, dicit homini: "Extende manum tuam." Et extendit, et restituta est manus illi.

6 Exeuntes autem pharisæi, statim cum Herodianis consilium faciebant adversus eum quomodo eum perderent.

7 Jesus autem cum discipulis suis secessit ad mare: et multa turba a Galilæa et Judæa secuta est eum, 8 et ab Jerosolymis, et ab Idumæa, et trans Jordanem: et qui circa Tyrum et Sidonem multitudo magna, audientes quæ faciebat, venerunt ad eum. 9 Et dicit discipulis suis ut navicula sibi deserviret propter turbam, ne comprimerent eum: 10 multos enim sanabat, ita ut irruerent in eum ut illum tangerent, quotquot habebant plagas.

11 Et spiritus immundi, cum illum videbant, procidebant ei: et clamabant, dicentes: "Tu es Filius Dei."

12 Et vehementer comminabatur eis ne manifestarent illum.

5 And looking around at them with anger, being grieved for the blindness of their hearts, he says to the man, "Stretch forth your hand." And he extended it, and his hand was restored to him. 6 And the Pharisees going out, immediately with the Herodians they were making a plan against him, how they might destroy him. 7 But Jesus retired with his disciples to the sea; and a great multitude followed him from Galilee and Judea, 8 And from Jerusalem, and from Idumea and from beyond the Jordan. And those from Tyre and Sidon, a great multitude, hearing which things he was doing, came to him. 9 And he spoke to his disciples that a small ship should wait for him, because of the multitude, lest they should crush him. 10 For he was healing many, so that they pressed upon him in order to touch him, as many as were having misfortunes. 11 And the unclean spirits, when they were seeing him, were falling down before him; and they were crying out, saying, 12 "You are the Son of God!" And he was strictly charging them that they should not make him known.

Mark 3:13-21

13 Et ascendens in montem vocavit ad se quos voluit ipse: et venerunt ad eum. 14 Et fecit ut essent duodecim cum illo: et ut mitteret eos prædicare. 15 Et dedit illis potestatem curandi infirmitates et ejiciendi dæmonia. 16 Et imposuit Simoni nomen Petrus: 17 et Jacobum Zebedæi, et Joannem fratrem Jacobi, et imposuit eis nomina Boanerges, quod est, Filii tonitrui: 18 et Andream, et Philippum, et Bartholomæum, et Matthæum, et Thomam, et Jacobum Alphæi, et Thaddæum, et Simonem Cananæum, 19 et Judam Iscariotem, qui et tradidit illum.

20 Et veniunt ad domum: et convenit iterum turba, ita ut non possent neque panem manducare.
21 Et cum audissent sui, exierunt tenere eum: dicebant enim: Quoniam in furorem versus est.

13 And going up into a mountain, he called to him those whom he himself wanted; and they came to him. 14 And he made that twelve would be with him, and that he would send them to preach. 15 And he gave them power to heal sicknesses and to cast out demons. 16 And to Simon he gave the name Peter; 17 And James the son of Zebedee, and John the brother of James; and he named them Boanerges, which is, The sons of thunder. 18 And Andrew and Philip, and Bartholomew and Matthew, and Thomas and James of Alpheus, and Thaddeus and Simon the Cananean; 19 And Judas Iscariot, who also betrayed him. 20 And they come to a house, and the multitude comes together again, so that thus they were not so much able even to eat bread. 21 And when his friends had heard of it, they went out to lay hold of him. For they were saying this: "He is turned mad!"

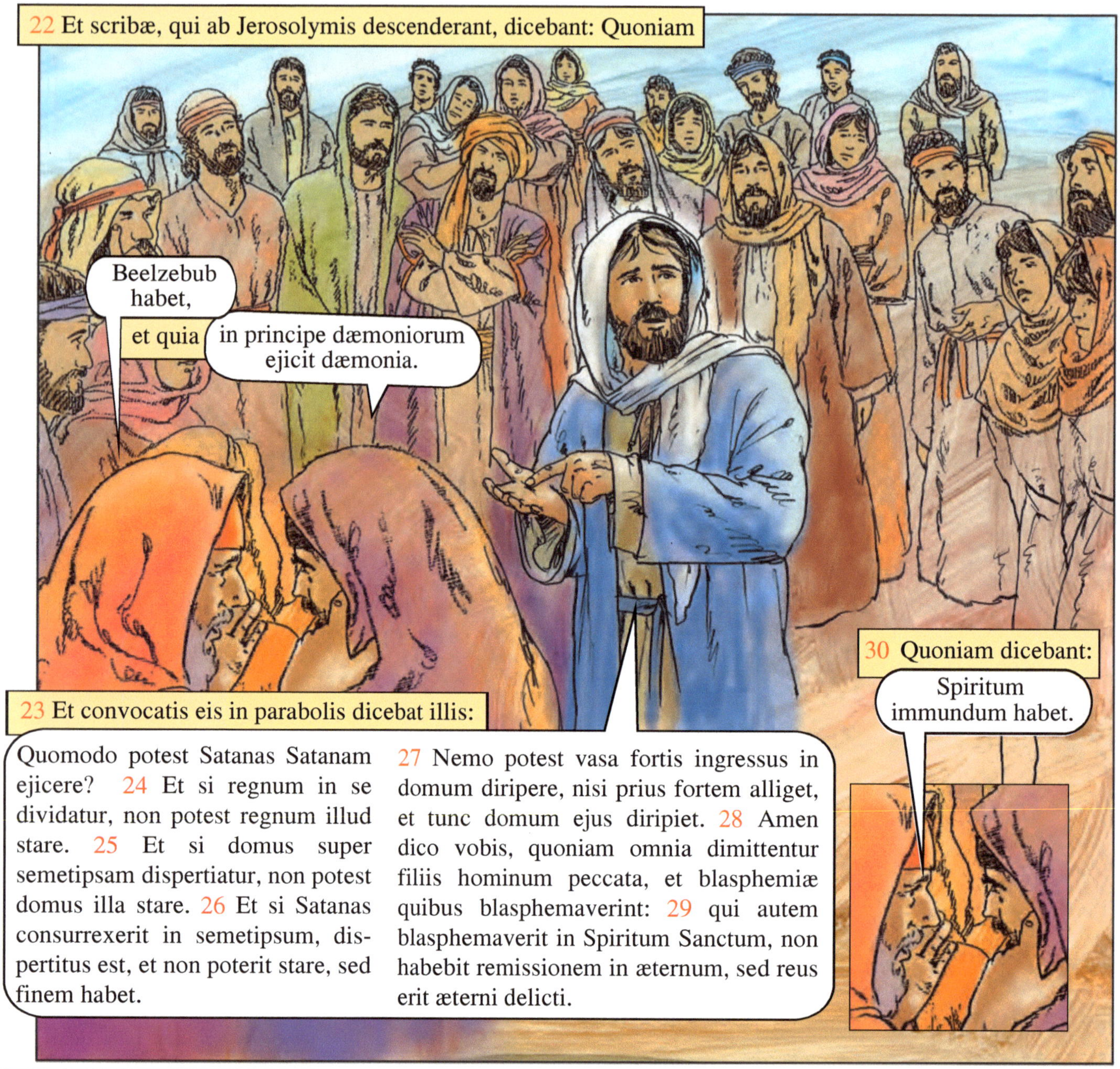

Mark 3:34-4:7

34 Et circumspiciens eos, qui in circuitu ejus sedebant, ait:

Ecce mater mea et fratres mei. 35 Qui enim fecerit voluntatem Dei, hic frater meus, et soror mea, et mater est.

Caput IV

1 Et iterum cœpit docere ad mare: et congregata est ad eum turba multa, ita ut navim ascendens sederet in mari, et omnis turba circa mare super terram erat: 2 et docebat eos in parabolis multa, et dicebat illis in doctrina sua:

4 Et dum seminat, aliud cecidit circa viam, et venerunt volucres cæli, et comederunt illud. 5 Aliud vero cecidit super petrosa, ubi non

terram multam: et statim exortum est, quoniam non habebat altitudinem terræ: 6 et quando exortus est sol,

exæstuavit: et eo quod non habebat radicem, exaruit.

7 Et aliud cecidit in spinas: et ascenderunt spinæ, et suffocaverunt illud, et fructum non dedit.

3 Audite: ecce exiit seminans ad seminandum.

34 And looking around at them who were sitting around him, he says, "Behold, my mother and my brothers! 35 For whoever does the will of God, this one is my brother, and my sister, and mother." 4:1 And again he began to teach by the sea side; and a great multitude was gathered together to him, so that thus climbing into a ship he sat in the sea, and all the multitude was on the land by the sea side. 2 And he was teaching them many things in parables and was saying to them in his teaching: 3 "Listen! Behold, the sower went out to sow. 4 And while he sowed, some fell by the wayside, and the birds of the air came and ate it. 5 And other some fell upon stony ground, where it had not much soil; and it shot up immediately, because it had no depth of soil. 6 And when the sun arose, it was scorched; and because it was not having a root, it withered away. 7 And some fell among thorns; and the thorns grew up, and choked it, and it yielded no fruit.

Mark 4:8-19

8 Et aliud cecidit in terram bonam: et dabat fructum ascendentem et crescentem, et afferebat unum triginta, unum sexaginta, et unum centum.

9 Et dicebat: Qui habet aures audiendi, audiat.

10 Et cum esset singularis, interrogaverunt eum hi qui cum eo erant duodecim, parabolam. 11 Et dicebat eis:

Vobis datum est nosse mysterium regni Dei: illis autem, qui foris sunt, in parabolis omnia fiunt:

12 ut videntes videant, et non videant: et audientes audiant, et non intelligant: nequando convertantur, et dimittantur eis peccata.

13 Et ait illis:

Nescitis parabolam hanc? Et quomodo omnes parabolas cognoscetis? 14 Qui seminat, verbum seminat.

15 Hi autem sunt, qui circa viam, ubi seminatur verbum, et cum audierint, confestim venit Satanas, et aufert verbum, quod seminatum est in cordibus eorum.

16 Et hi sunt similiter, qui super petrosa seminantur: qui cum audierint verbum, statim cum gaudio accipiunt illud:

17 et non habent radicem in se, sed temporales sunt:

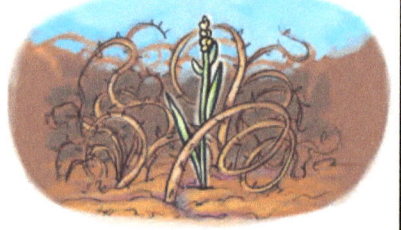

deinde orta tribulatione et persecutione propter verbum, confestim scandalizantur. 18 Et alii sunt qui in spinas seminantur: hi sunt qui verbum audiunt, 19 et ærumnæ sæculi, et deceptio divitiarum, et circa reliqua concupiscentiæ introëuntes suffocant verbum, et sine fructu efficitur.

8 And some fell upon good ground; and they were bringing forth fruit growing up and increasing, and they were yielding, one thirty, another sixty, and another a hundred." 9 And he was saying, "He that has ears to hear, let him hear!" 10 And when he was alone, the twelve who were with him asked him the parable. 11 And he was saying to them, "To you it is given to know the mystery of the kingdom of God; but to them who are outside, all things occur in parables; 12 so that seeing they would see, and not perceive; and hearing they would hear, and not understand; lest at any time they be converted, and their sins be forgiven them." 13 And he says to them, "Are you ignorant of this parable? And how will you know all parables? 14 He who sows, sows the word. 15 And these are they by the wayside, where the word is sown, and as soon as they have heard, immediately Satan comes and takes away the word that was sown in their hearts. 16 And these likewise are they that are sown on the stony ground; who when they have heard the word, immediately receive it with joy. 17 And they have no root in themselves, but are temporary; and then when tribulation and persecution arise on account of the word, they are immediately scandalized. 18 And the others there who are sown among thorns; these are they that hear the word, 19 And the cares of the world, and the deceitfulness of riches, and the lusts after other things entering in choke the word, and it is made fruitless.

Mark 4:20-34

20 Et hi sunt qui super terram bonam seminati sunt, qui audiunt verbum, et suscipiunt, et fructificant, unum triginta, unum sexaginta, et unum centum

21 Et dicebat illis:

Numquid venit lucerna ut sub modio ponatur, aut sub lecto? nonne ut super candelabrum ponatur? 22 Non est enim aliquid absconditum, quod non manifestetur: nec factum est occultum, sed ut in palam veniat. 23 Si quis habet aures audiendi, audiat.

24 Et dicebat illis: Videte quid audiatis. In qua mensura mensi fueritis, remetietur vobis, et adjicietur vobis. 25 Qui enim habet, dabitur illi: et qui non habet, etiam quod habet auferetur ab eo.

26 Et dicebat:

Sic est regnum Dei, quemadmodum si homo jaciat sementem in terram, 27 et dormiat, et exsurgat nocte et die, et semen germinet, et increscat dum nescit ille. 28 Ultro enim terra fructificat, primum herbam, deinde spicam, deinde plenum frumentum in spica.

29 Et cum produxerit fructus, statim mittit falcem, quoniam adest messis.

30 Et dicebat:

Cui assimilabimus regnum Dei? aut cui parabolæ comparabimus illud? 31 Sicut granum sinapis, quod cum seminatum fuerit in terra, minus est omnibus seminibus, quæ sunt in terra: 32 et cum seminatum fuerit, ascendit, et fit majus omnibus oleribus, et facit ramos magnos, ita ut possint sub umbra ejus aves cæli habitare.

33 Et talibus multis parabolis loquebatur eis verbum, prout poterant audire: 34 sine parabola autem non loquebatur eis: seorsum autem discipulis suis disserebat omnia.

20 And these are they who are sown upon the good ground, who hear the word, and receive it, and yield fruit, the one thirty, another sixty, and another a hundred." 21 And he was saying to them, "A candle doesn't come in to be put under a bushel, or under a bed, does it? (No.) And Is it not to be set on a candlestick? (Yes.) 22 For there is nothing hid, which will not be made manifest; neither was it made secret, but that it will come in the open. 23 If anyone has ears to hear, let him hear!" 24 And he was saying to them, "Take heed what you hear. By what measure you will measure, it will be measured to you again, and more will be given to you. 25 For he that has, to him will be given; and he that has not, that also which he has will be taken away from him." 26 And he was saying, "Thus is the kingdom of God, just as if a person should cast seed into the soil, 27 And should sleep, and rise, night and day, and the seed should germinate, and grow up while he does not know. 28 For the earth of itself brings forth fruit, first the blade, then the ear, afterwards the full corn in the ear. 29 And when the fruit is brought forth, immediately he puts in the sickle, because the harvest is come." 30 And he was saying, "To what shall we liken the kingdom of God? Or with what parable shall we compare it? 31 It is like a grain of mustard seed, which when it is sown in the ground, is less than all the seeds that are in the ground; 32 and when it is sown, it grows up, and becomes greater than all herbs, and sprouts out great branches, so that thus the birds of the air are able to dwell under the shadow of it." 33 And with many such parables he was speaking to them the word, according as they were able to hear. 34 And without parable he was not speaking to them; but apart, he was explaining all things to his disciples.

Mark 4:35-39a

35 And he says to them that day when evening had come, "Let us pass over to the other side." 36 And sending away the multitude, they take him so that thus he was in the ship; and there were other ships with him. 37 And a great storm of wind occurred, and the waves were beating against the ship, so that thus the ship was filled. 38 And he himself was at the back of the ship sleeping on a pillow; and they awake him, and say to him, "Teacher, does it not concern you that we are perishing?!" 39a And rising up, he rebuked the wind, and said to the sea, "Peace, be still!"

Mark 4:39b-5:11

Et cessavit ventus: et facta est tranquillitas magna.

40 Et ait illis:
Quid timidi estis? necdum habetis fidem?

et timuerunt timore magno, et dicebant ad alterutrum:
Quis, putas, est iste, quia et ventus et mare obediunt ei?

Caput V

1 Et venerunt trans fretum maris in regionem Gerasenorum. 2 Et exeunti ei de navi, statim occurrit de monumentis homo in spiritu immundo, 3 qui domicilium habebat in monumentis, et neque catenis jam quisquam poterat eum ligare: 4 quoniam sæpe compedibus et catenis vinctus, dirupisset catenas, et compedes comminuisset, et nemo poterat eum domare:

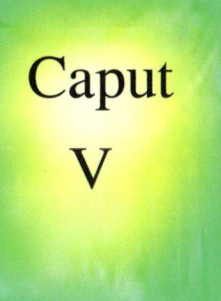

5 et semper die ac nocte in monumentis, et in montibus erat, clamans, et concidens se lapidibus.

6 Videns autem Jesum a longe, cucurrit, et adoravit eum: 7 et clamans voce magna dixit:
Quid mihi et tibi, Jesu Fili Dei altissimi? adjuro te per Deum, ne me torqueas.

8 Dicebat enim illi:
Exi spiritus immunde ab homine.

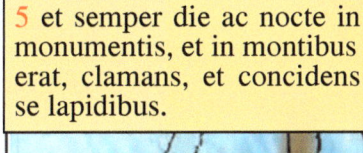

9 Et interrogabat eum:
Quod tibi nomen est?
Et dicit ei:
Legio mihi nomen est, quia multi sumus.

10 Et deprecabatur eum multum, ne se expelleret extra regionem. 11 Erat autem ibi circa montem grex porcorum magnus, pascens.

39b And the wind ceased; and a great calm was made. 40 And he said to them, "Why are you fearful? Don't you have faith yet?" And they feared with a great fear, and they were saying to one another, "Who, do you think, is this that both wind and sea obey him?!" 5:1 And they came over the strait of the sea into the country of the Gerasenes. 2 And as he exited from the ship, immediately a person from the tombs with an unclean spirit runs up, 3 who was having his dwelling in the tombs, and not even with chains was anyone able to bind him. 4 For having been often bound with fetters and chains, he had broken the chains, and shattered the fetters, and no one was able to tame him. 5 And he was always day and night in the tombs and in the mountains, crying and cutting himself with stones. 6 And seeing Jesus a long way off, he runs and paid him homage. 7 And crying with a loud voice, he says, "What (is there) between me and you, Jesus the Son of the most high God? I adjure you by God that you do not torment me!" 8 For he was saying to him, "Come out from the person, you unclean spirit!" 9 And he was asking him, "What is your name?" And he says to him, "My name is Legion, because we are many." 10 And he was begging him much, that he would not drive him away out of the country. 11 And there was near the mountain a great herd of swine, feeding.

Mark 5:12-21

12 And the spirits were begging him, saying, "Send us into the swine, so that we may enter into them." 13 And Jesus immediately grants them leave. And the unclean spirits going out, entered into the swine; and the herd with great violence was carried headlong into the sea, being about two thousand, and they were suffocated in the sea. 14 And the one who were feeding them fled, and told it in the city and in the fields. And they went out to see what had happened. 15 And they came to Jesus, and they see him who was troubled from the demon, sitting, clothed, and with a sane mind, and they were afraid. 16 And the ones who had seen it, told them in what manner it had happened to him who had the demon, and concerning the swine. 17 And they began to implore him that he would depart from their coasts. 18 And when he went up into the ship, he who had been troubled with the demon, began to beg him that he would be with him. 19 And he did not admit him, but says to him, "Go in your house to your friends, and tell them what great things the Lord has done for you, and has had mercy on you." 20 And he went his way, and began to proclaim in Decapolis what great things Jesus had done for him; and all were marveling. 21 And when Jesus had passed again in the ship over the strait, a great multitude assembled together to him, and he was near the sea.

Mark 5:22-30a

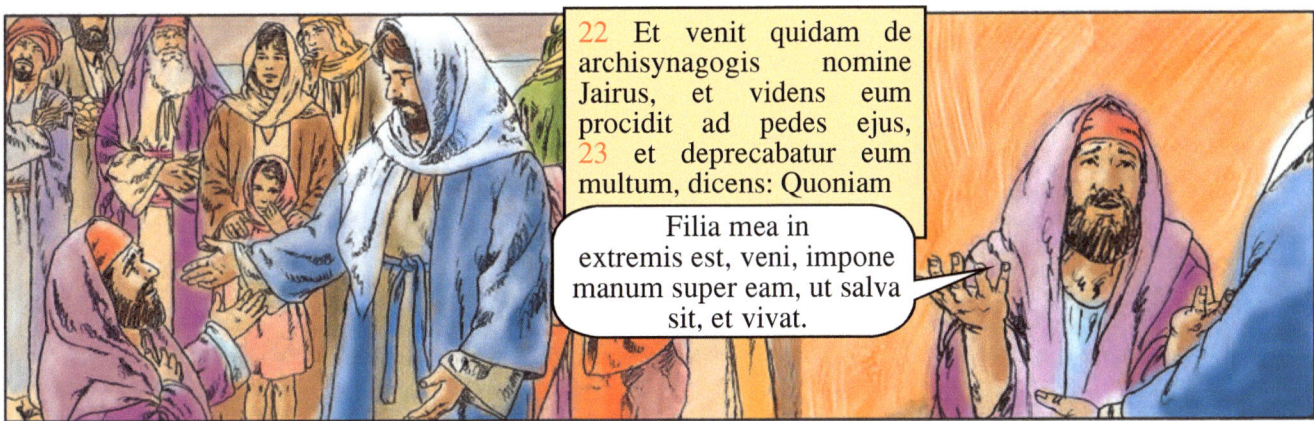

22 Et venit quidam de archisynagogis nomine Jairus, et videns eum procidit ad pedes ejus, 23 et deprecabatur eum multum, dicens: Quoniam

Filia mea in extremis est, veni, impone manum super eam, ut salva sit, et vivat.

24 Et abiit cum illo, et sequebatur eum turba multa, et comprimebant eum. 25 Et mulier, quæ erat in profluvio sanguinis annis duodecim, 26 et fuerat multa perpessa a compluribus medicis:

et erogaverat omnia sua, nec quidquam profecerat, sed magis deterius habebat: 27 cum audisset de Jesu, venit in turba retro, et tetigit vestimentum ejus: 28 dicebat enim: Quia

Si vel vestimentum ejus tetigero, salva ero.

29 Et confestim siccatus est fons sanguinis ejus: et sensit corpore quia sanata esset a plaga.
30 Et statim Jesus in semetipso cognoscens virtutem quæ exierat de illo,

22 And there comes one of the rulers of the synagogue named Jairus; and seeing him, falls down at his feet. 23 And he was begging him much, saying this: "My daughter is at the point of death, come, lay your hand upon her, so that she may be safe, and may live!" 24 And he went with him, and a great multitude was following him, and they were crowding him. 25 And a woman who was under an issue of blood twelve years, 26 And had suffered many things from many physicians; and had spent all that she had, nor was anything better, but she was rather having it worse, 27 When she had heard of Jesus, comes in the crowd behind him, and touched his garment. 28 For she was saying this: "If I will touch even his garment, I will be whole." 29 And immediately the fountain of her blood was dried up, and she felt in her body that she was healed of the malady. 30a And immediately Jesus knowing in himself the power that had gone out from him,

Mark 5:30b-40a

30b turning to the multitude, was saying, "Who touched my garments?" 31 And his disciples were saying to him, "You see the multitude crowding you, and you say, 'who touched me?'!" 32 And he was looking around to see her who had done this. 33 But the woman fearing and trembling, knowing what had occurred in her, came and fell down before him, and told him all the truth. 34 And he said to her, "Daughter, your faith has made you whole; go in peace, and be healthy from your malady!" 35 While he was yet speaking, some come from the ruler of the synagogue's house, saying this: "Your daughter is dead; why do you trouble the master any further?" 36 But Jesus having heard the word that was spoken, says to the ruler of the synagogue, "Fear not, only believe!" 37 And he did not admit anyone to follow him, but Peter, and James, and John the brother of James. 38 And they come to the house of the ruler of the synagogue; and he sees a tumult, and people weeping and wailing much. 39 And going in, he says to them, "Why are you disturbed, and weeping? The girl is not dead, but sleeps." 40a And they were laughing at him.

Mark 5:40b-6:2

Caput VI

40b But he having them all put out, takes the father and the mother of the girl, and those who were with him, and enters in where the girl was lying. 41 And taking the girl by the hand, he says to her, "Talitha cumi," which is interpreted: "Young girl, (I say to you) arise!" 42 And immediately the girl arose, and was walking; and she was twelve years old; and they were astonished with a great astonishment. 43 And he charged them strictly that no one should know it; and he said that something should be given her to eat. 6:1 And going out from there, he went into his own country; and his disciples were following him. 2 And when the Sabbath came, he began to teach in the synagogue; and many hearing him were admiring at his teaching, saying, "From where (comes) to this guy all these things? And what wisdom is this that is given to him, and such mighty works as are accomplished by his hands?

Mark 6:3-13

3 Is this not the carpenter, the son of Mary, the brother of James, and Joseph, and Jude, and Simon? (Yes.) Are not also his sisters here with us? (Yes.)" And they were being scandalized by him. 4 And Jesus was saying to them this: "A prophet is not without honor, but in his own country, and in his own house, and among his own kindred." 5 And he was not able to do any miracles there, except laying his hands he cured a few that were sick. 6 And he was marveling at their unbelief, and he was circulating among the villages in a circuit teaching. 7 And he called the twelve; and began to send them two and two, and was giving them power over unclean spirits. 8 And he commanded them that they should take nothing for the way, but a staff only; no bag, no bread, nor money in their purse, 9 But to be fitted with sandals, and that they should not put on two coats. 10 And he was saying to them, "Wherever you will enter into a house, there stay until you depart from that place. 11 And whosoever will not receive you, nor hear you; going forth from there, shake off the dust from your feet as a testimony to them. 12 And going forth they were preaching that they should be making repentance; 13 and they were casting out many demons, and anointing with oil many that were sick, and were healing them.

Mark 6:14-23

14 And king Herod heard (for his name was made manifest) and he was saying this: "John the Baptist has risen again from dead, and therefore mighty deeds are working in him." 15 And others were saying this: "He is Elijah." But others were saying this: "He is a prophet, just like one of the prophets." 16 Which hearing, Herod said, "John whom I beheaded, this man is risen again from the dead!" 17 For Herod himself had sent and apprehended John, and bound him prison for the sake of Herodias the wife of Philip his brother, because he had married her. 18 For John was saying to Herod, "It is not lawful for you to have your brother's wife." 19 Now Herodias was laying a trap for him and was desirous to put him to death yet was not able. 20 For Herod was fearing John, knowing him to be a righteous and holy man; and he was keeping him, and when hearing him, he was doing many things and he was gladly listening to him. 21 And when a convenient day came, Herod made a supper for his birthday, for the princes, and tribunes, and chief men of Galilee. 22 And when the daughter of the same Herodias had come in, and had danced, and pleased Herod, and them that were at table with him, the king said to the girl, "Ask of me what you want, and I will give it to you." 23 And he swore to her this: "Whatsoever you will ask I will give you; half of my kingdom is permitted!"

Mark 6:24-33

24 Who when she went out, said to her mother, "What should I ask?" But her mother said, "The head of John the Baptist." 25 And when she had come in immediately with haste to the king, she asked, saying, "I want that immediately you give me in a dish the head of John the Baptist." 26 And the king was saddened; because of his oath, and because of those who were with him at table, he was unwilling to displease her. 27 But sending an executioner, he commanded that his head should be brought in a dish. And he beheaded him in the prison, 28 and brought his head in a dish; and gave to the girl, and the girl gave it her mother. 29 With this heard, his disciples came and took his body, and laid it in a tomb. 30 And the apostles, coming together to Jesus, related to him all things that they had done and taught. 31 And he says to them, "Come apart into a desert place, and rest a little." For there were many who were coming and were going; and they were not having time to eat. 32 And going up into a ship, they went into a desert place apart. 33 And they saw them going away, and many knew; and they on foot from all the cities ran there, and they went on before them.

Mark 6:34-40

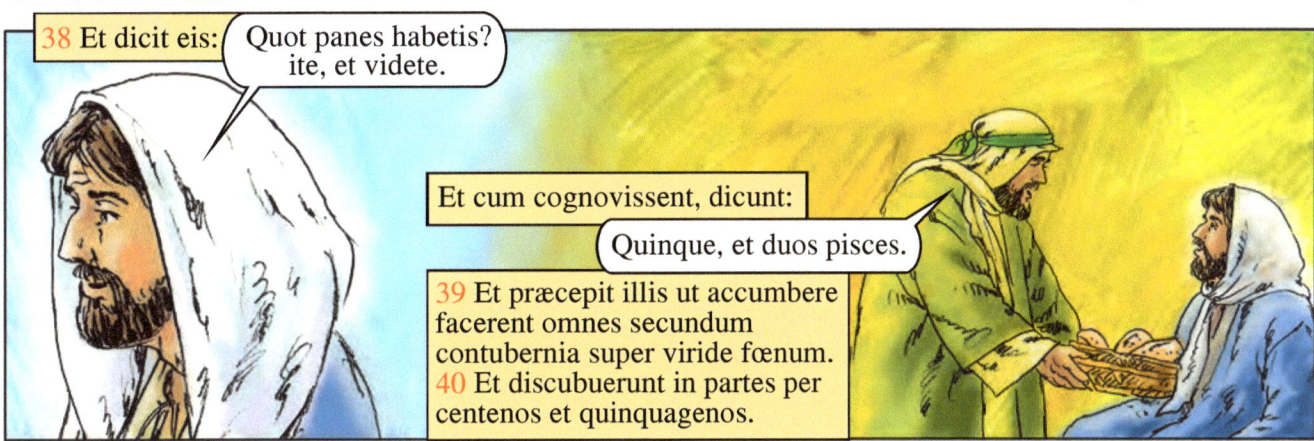

34 And Jesus going out saw a great multitude; and he had compassion on them, because they were as sheep not having a shepherd, and he began to teach them many things. 35 And when the day was now far spent, his disciples came to him, saying, "This is a desert place, and the hour is now past; 36 send them away, so that going into the next villages and towns, they may buy themselves meat which they may eat." 37 And answering back, he said to them, "You yourselves give them (something) to eat." And they said to him, "Let us go and buy bread for two hundred pence, and we will give them (something) to eat." 38 And he says to them, "How many loaves do you have? Go, and see." And when they knew, they say, "Five, and two fishes." 39 And he commanded them that they should make them all sit down by companies upon the green grass. 40 And they sat down in ranks, by hundreds and by fifties.

Mark 6:41-44

41 Et acceptis quinque panibus et duobus piscibus, intuens in cælum, benedixit, et fregit panes, et dedit discipulis suis, ut ponerent ante eos: et duos pisces divisit omnibus.

42 Et manducaverunt omnes, et saturati sunt. 43 Et sustulerunt reliquias, fragmentorum duodecim cophinos plenos, et de piscibus. 44 Erant autem qui manducaverunt quinque millia virorum.

41 And when he had taken the five loaves and the two fishes, looking up to heaven, he blessed, and broke the loaves, and gave to his disciples so that they would set before them; and the two fishes he divided for them all. 42 And they all ate, and were well-fed. 43 And they took up the remnants, twelve full baskets of fragments, and of the fishes. 44 Moreover, they who ate were five thousand men

Mark 6:45-55

45 Et statim coëgit discipulos suos ascendere navim, ut præcederent eum trans fretum ad Bethsaidam, dum ipse dimitteret populum.

46 Et cum dimisisset eos, abiit in montem orare.

47 Et cum sero esset, erat navis in medio mari et ipse solus in terra.
48 Et videns eos laborantes in remigando (erat enim ventus contrarius eis) et circa quartam vigiliam noctis venit ad eos ambulans supra mare: et volebat præterire eos.

49 At illi ut viderunt eum ambulantem supra mare, putaverunt phantasma esse, et exclamaverunt.
50 Omnes enim viderunt eum, et conturbati sunt. Et statim locutus est cum eis, et dixit eis:

Confidite, ego sum: nolite timere.

51 Et ascendit ad illos in navim, et cessavit ventus. Et plus magis intra se stupebant: 52 non enim intellexerunt de panibus: erat enim cor eorum obcæcatum.

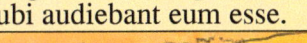

53 Et cum transfretassent, venerunt in terram Genesareth, et applicuerunt. 54 Cumque egressi essent de navi, continuo cognoverunt eum: 55 et percurrentes universam regionem illam, cœperunt in grabatis eos, qui se male habebant, circumferre, ubi audiebant eum esse.

45 And immediately he compelled his disciples to go up into the ship, so that they would go before him over the water to Bethsaida, while he himself dismissed the people. 46 And when he had dismissed them, he went up to the mountain to pray. 47 And when it was late, the ship was in the midst of the sea, and himself alone on the land. 48 And seeing them laboring in rowing (for the wind was against them), and about the fourth watch of the night, he comes to them walking upon the sea, and he was wanting to pass by them. 49 But they, when they saw him walking upon the sea, thought it was a ghost, and they cried out. 50 For they all saw him, and were troubled. And immediately he spoke with them, and said to them, "Have confidence! It is I; fear not!" 51 And he went up to them into the ship, and the wind ceased. And they were far more marveling among themselves; 52 for they did not understand about the loaves; for their heart was blinded. 53 And when they had passed over, they came into the land of Genezareth, and landed. 54 And when they had gone out of the ship, immediately they recognized him; 55 and running through that whole country, they were carrying about in beds those who were having it badly, where they were hearing that he was.

Mark 6:56-7:8

56 Et quocumque introibat, in vicos, vel in villas aut civitates, in plateis ponebant infirmos, et deprecabantur eum, ut vel fimbriam vestimenti ejus tangerent, et quotquot tangebant eum, salvi fiebant.

Caput VII

1 Et conveniunt ad eum pharisæi, et quidam de scribis, venientes ab Jerosolymis. 2 Et cum vidissent quosdam ex discipulis ejus communibus manibus, id est non lotis, manducare panes, vituperaverunt. 3 Pharisæi enim, et omnes Judæi, nisi crebro laverint manus, non manducant, tenentes traditionem seniorum: 4 et a foro nisi baptizentur, non comedunt: et alia multa sunt, quæ tradita sunt illis servare, baptismata calicum, et urceorum, et æramentorum, et lectorum: 5 et interrogabant eum pharisæi et scribæ:

Quare discipuli tui non ambulant juxta traditionem seniorum, sed communibus manibus manducant panem?

6 At ille respondens, dixit eis:

Bene prophetavit Isaias de vobis hypocritis, sicut scriptum est:

Populus hic labiis me honorat, cor autem eorum longe est a me: 7 in vanum autem me colunt, docentes doctrinas, et præcepta hominum.

8 Relinquentes enim mandatum Dei, tenetis traditionem hominum, baptismata urceorum et calicum: et alia similia his facitis multa.

56 And wherever he was entering, into towns or into villages or cities, they were laying the sick in the streets, and were asking him that they might touch but the hem of his garment; and as many as were touching him were being made whole. 7:1 And Pharisees assembled together to him, and some of the scribes, coming from Jerusalem. 2 And when they had seen some of his disciples eat bread with common, that is, with unwashed hands, they found fault. 3 For the Pharisees, and all the Jews, do not eat unless repeatedly they washed their hands, holding the tradition of the elders. 4 And (coming) from the market, unless they are washed, they do not eat; and there are many other things that have been delivered to them to observe—the washings of cups and of pots and of brazen vessels and of beds. 5 And the Pharisees and scribes were asking him, "Why do not your disciples walk according to the tradition of the elders, but they eat bread with ordinary (unwashed) hands?" 6 But he, answering back, said to them, "Well did Isaiah prophesy of you hypocrites, just as it is written, 'This people honor me with their lips, but their heart is far from me. 7 Moreover, in vain do they worship me, teaching doctrines and precepts of men.' 8 For leaving the commandment of God, you hold the tradition of people—the washing of pots and of cups; and many other things like these you do."

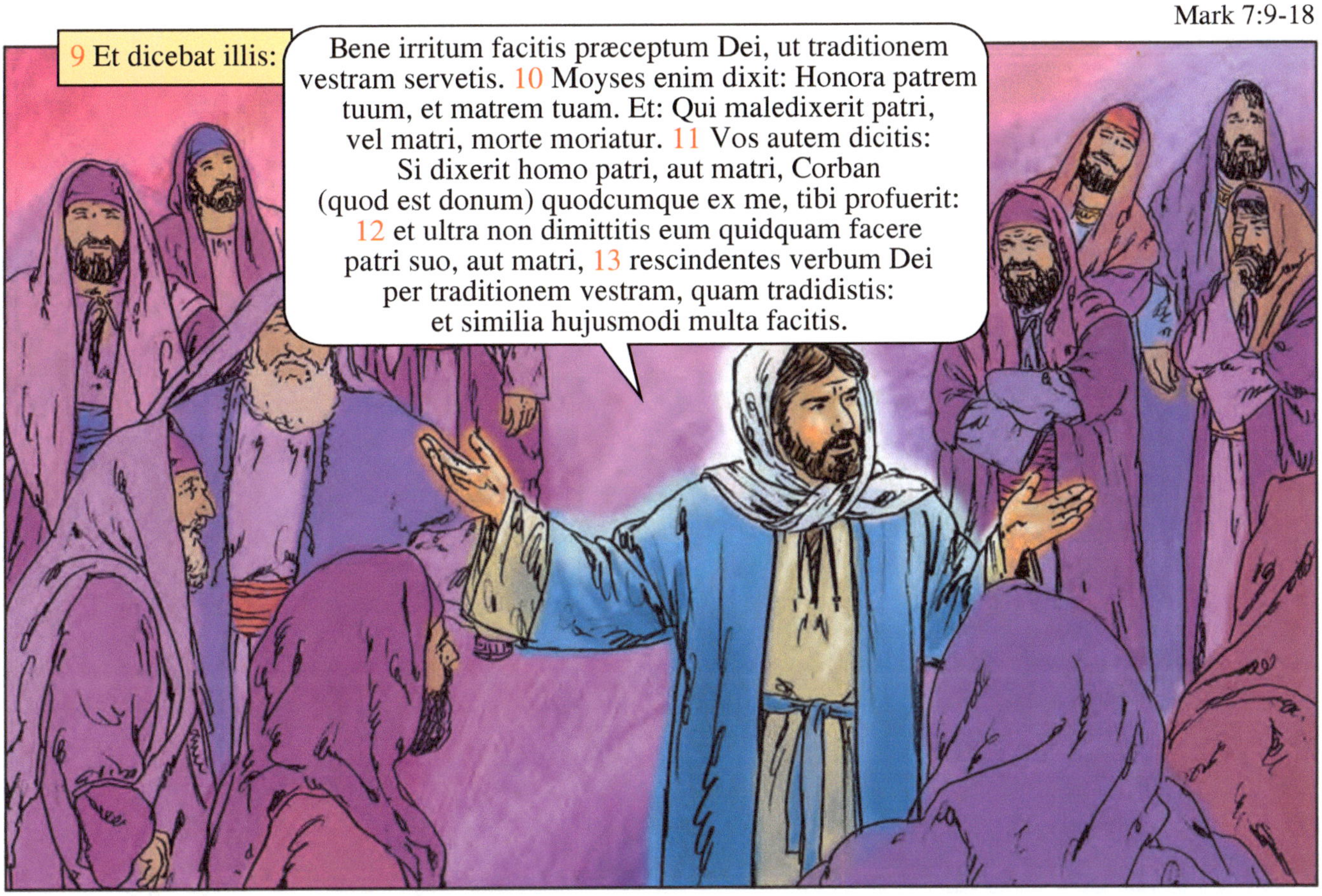

Mark 7:19-28

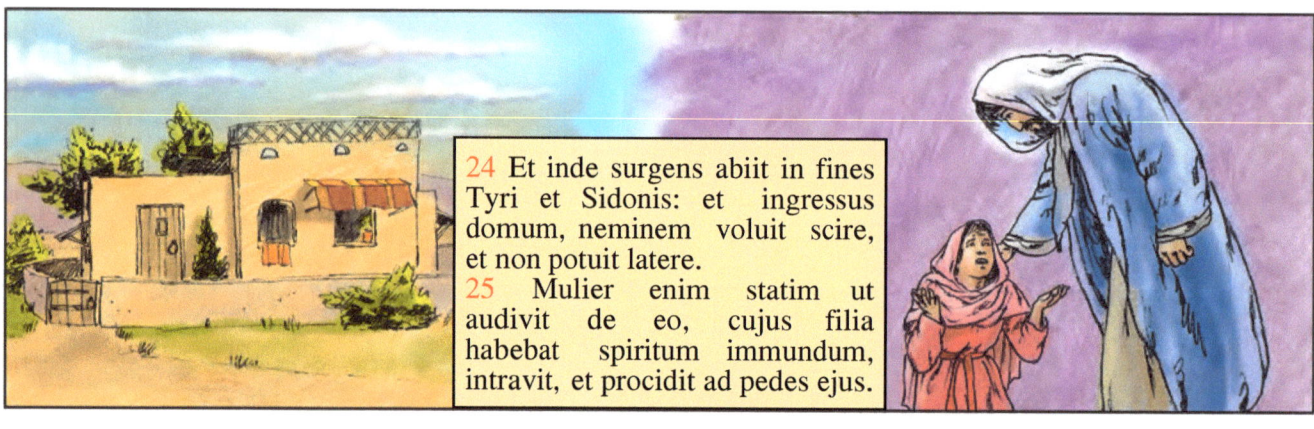

Mark 7:29-37

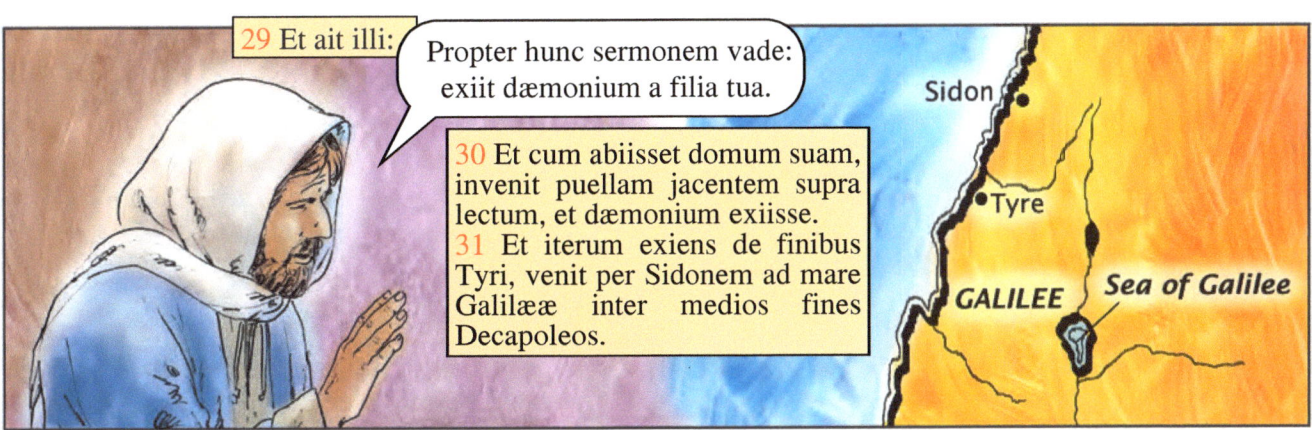

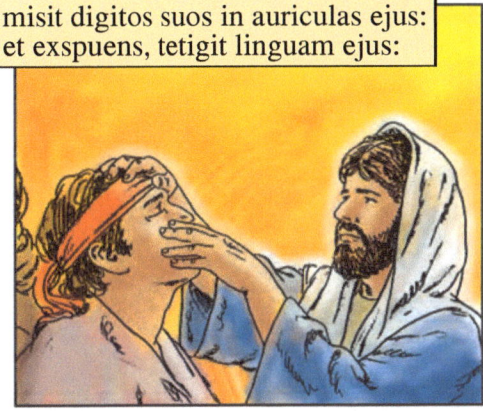

29 And he said to her, "Because of this word, go; the demon is gone out of your daughter." 30 And when she departed to her house, she found the girl lying upon the bed and that the demon was gone out. 31 And again going down the coasts of Tyre, he came by Sidon to the sea of Galilee through the middle boundaries of the Decapolis. 32 And they are bringing to him a deaf person and mute, and they were asking him that he would lay his hand upon him. 33 And taking him from the multitude separately, he put his fingers into his ears; and spitting, he touched his tongue. 34 And looking up to heaven, he groaned and said to him, "Ephpheta!" which is, "Be opened!" 35 And immediately his ears were opened and the bond of his tongue was loosed and he was speaking correctly. 36 And he charged them that they should tell no one. But the more he was charging them, so much more greatly they were proclaiming it! 37 And so much more they were marveling at him, saying, "He has done all things well! He both has made the deaf to hear and the mute to speak!"

Mark 8:1-9

Caput VIII

1 In diebus illis iterum cum turba multa esset, nec haberent quod manducarent, convocatis discipulis, ait illis:

2 Misereor super turbam: quia ecce jam triduo sustinent me, nec habent quod manducent: 3 et si dimisero eos jejunos in domum suam, deficient in via: quidam enim ex eis de longe venerunt.

4 Et responderunt ei discipuli sui:

Unde illos quis poterit saturare panibus in solitudine?

5 Et interrogavit eos:

Quot panes habetis?

Qui dixerunt:

Septem.

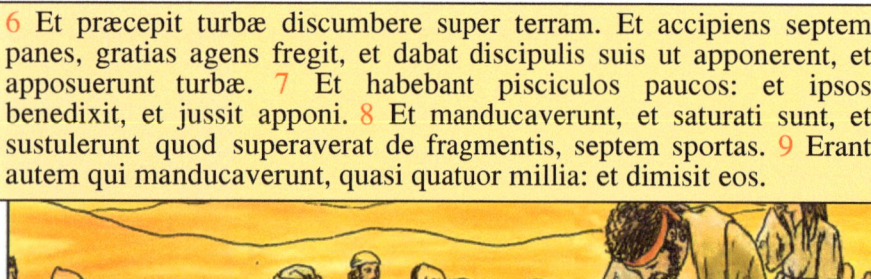

6 Et præcepit turbæ discumbere super terram. Et accipiens septem panes, gratias agens fregit, et dabat discipulis suis ut apponerent, et apposuerunt turbæ. 7 Et habebant pisciculos paucos: et ipsos benedixit, et jussit apponi. 8 Et manducaverunt, et saturati sunt, et sustulerunt quod superaverat de fragmentis, septem sportas. 9 Erant autem qui manducaverunt, quasi quatuor millia: et dimisit eos.

8:1 In those days again, when there was a great multitude and they had nothing that they could eat, calling his disciples together, he says to them: 2 "I am having compassion concerning the multitude, for behold they have now been with me three days and have nothing to eat. 3 And if I should send them away fasting to their home, they will faint in the way; for some of them came from afar." 4 And his disciples responded back to him, "From where is anyone able to satisfy them here with bread in the wilderness?" 5 And he asked them, "How many loaves do you have?" Who said, "Seven." 6 And he commanded the people to sit down on the ground. And taking the seven loaves, giving thanks, he broke and was giving to his disciples so that they would serve (them). And they served them for the people. 7 And they were having a few little fishes; and he blessed them and commanded (them) to be served. 8 And they ate and were satisfied; and they took up that which was left of the fragments, —seven baskets. 9 And they who had eaten were about four thousand; and he sent them away.

10 And immediately going up into a ship with his disciples, he came into the parts of Dalmanutha. 11 And the Pharisees came forth and began to question with him, asking him a sign from heaven, tempting him. 12 And sighing deeply in spirit, he says, "Why does this generation seek a sign? Amen! I say to you, a sign will not be given to this generation!" 13 And leaving them, he went up again into the ship and passed to the other side of the water. 14 And they forgot to take bread; and they were having but one loaf with them in the ship. 15 And he was charging them saying, "Take heed, and beware of the leaven of the Pharisees and of the leaven of Herod!" 16 And they were reasoning among themselves, saying this: "Because we have no bread." 17 Which begin known, Jesus says to them, "Why do you reason, because you have no bread? Do you not yet know nor understand? Do you still have your heart blinded? 18 Having eyes, are you not seeing? And having ears, are you not hearing? Neither are you remembering? 19 When I broke the five loaves among five thousand, how many baskets full of fragments did you take up?" They say to him, "Twelve." 20 "When also the seven loaves among four thousand, how many baskets of fragments did you take up?" And they say to him, "Seven." 21 And he was saying to them, "How are you not yet understanding?!"

Mark 8:31-39

31 Et cœpit docere eos quoniam oportet Filium hominis pati multa, et reprobari a senioribus, et a summis sacerdotibus et scribis, et occidi: et post tres dies resurgere.
32 Et palam verbum loquebatur. Et apprehendens eum Petrus, cœpit increpare eum.

33 Qui conversus, et videns discipulos suos, comminatus est Petro, dicens:

Vade retro me Satana, quoniam non sapis quæ Dei sunt, sed quæ sunt hominum.

34 Et convocata turba cum discipulis suis, dixit eis:

Si quis vult me sequi, deneget semetipsum: et tollat crucem suam, et sequatur me. 35 Qui enim voluerit animam suam salvam facere, perdet eam: qui autem perdiderit animam suam propter me, et Evangelium, salvam faciet eam.
36 Quid enim proderit homini, si lucretur mundum totum et detrimentum animæ suæ faciat?
37 Aut quid dabit homo commutationis pro anima sua?
38 Qui enim me confusus fuerit, et verba mea in generatione ista adultera et peccatrice, et Filius hominis confundetur eum, cum venerit in gloria Patris sui cum angelis sanctis.

39 Et dicebat illis:

Amen dico vobis, quia sunt quidam de hic stantibus, qui non gustabunt mortem donec videant regnum Dei veniens in virtute.

31 And he began to teach them that the Son of Humanity must suffer many things, and be rejected by the elders and by the high priests and the scribes, and be killed; and after three days rise again. 32 And he was speaking the word openly. And taking him Peter began to rebuke him. 33 Who turning about and seeing his disciples, threatened Peter, saying, "Go behind me, Satan, because you do not have in mind the things that are of God but that are of humans." 34 And with the multitude called together with his disciples, he said to them, "If anyone will follow me, let him deny himself and take up his cross and follow me. 35 For whosoever will save his life will lose it; and whosoever will lose his life for my sake and the gospel will save it. 36 For what will it profit a person, if he gains the whole world and suffers the loss of his soul? 37 Or what will a person give in exchange for his soul? 38 For he who will be ashamed of me and of my words in this adulterous and sinful generation, also the Son of Humanity will be ashamed of him, when he will come in the glory of his Father with the holy angels." 39 And he was saying to them, "Amen! I say to you that there are some from the ones standing here, who will not taste death until they see the kingdom of God coming in power."

Mark 9:1-12

Caput IX

1 Et post dies sex assumit Jesus Petrum, et Jacobum, et Joannem, et ducit illos in montem excelsum seorsum solos, et transfiguratus est coram ipsis. 2 Et vestimenta ejus facta sunt splendentia, et candida nimis velut nix, qualia fullo non potest super terram candida facere. 3 Et apparuit illis Elias cum Moyse: et erant loquentes cum Jesu.

4 Et respondens Petrus, ait Jesu:

Rabbi, bonum est nos hic esse: et faciamus tria tabernacula, tibi unum, et Moysi unum, et Eliæ unum.

5 Non enim sciebat quid diceret: erant enim timore exterriti.

6 Et facta est nubes obumbrans eos: et venit vox de nube, dicens:

Hic est Filius meus carissimus: audite illum.

7 Et statim circumspicientes, neminem amplius viderunt, nisi Jesum tantum secum.

8 Et descendentibus illis de monte, præcepit illis ne cuiquam quæ vidissent, narrarent: nisi cum Filius hominis a mortuis resurrexerit. 9 Et verbum continuerunt apud se: conquirentes quid esset, cum a mortuis resurrexerit.

10 Et interrogabant eum, dicentes:

Quid ergo dicunt pharisæi et scribæ, quia Eliam oportet venire primum?

11 Qui respondens, ait illis:

Elias cum venerit primo, restituet omnia: et quomodo scriptum est in Filium hominis, ut multa patiatur et contemnatur. 12 Sed dico vobis quia et Elias venit (et fecerunt illi quæcumque voluerunt) sicut scriptum est de eo.

9:1 And after six days, Jesus takes with him Peter and James and John, and leads them up into a high mountain apart by themselves, and was transfigured before them. 2 And his garments became shining and exceeding white as snow, so as no launderer upon earth can make white. 3 And Elijah with Moses appeared to them; and they were talking with Jesus. 4 And Peter responding, says to Jesus, "Rabbi, it is good for us to be here. And let us make three tabernacles, one for you, and one for Moses, and one for Elijah." 5 For he was not knowing what he was saying; for they were struck with fear. 6 And there was a cloud overshadowing them. And a voice came out of the cloud, saying, "This is my most beloved Son; listen to him!" 7 And immediately looking about, they saw no one any more, except Jesus only with them. 8 And as they were coming down from the mountain, he charged them not to tell anyone what things they had seen; until when the Son of Humanity will be risen from the dead. 9 And they kept the word to themselves; questioning together what it is (meaning) when he will be risen from the dead. 10 And they were asking him, saying, "Why therefore do the Pharisees and scribes say that Elijah needs to come first?" 11 Who answering, said to them, "Elijah, when he will come first, will restore all things; and as it is written of the Son of Humanity that he must suffer many things and be despised. 12 But I am saying to you that Elijah also came (and they have done to him whatsoever they would), just as it is written concerning him."

Mark 9:13-22

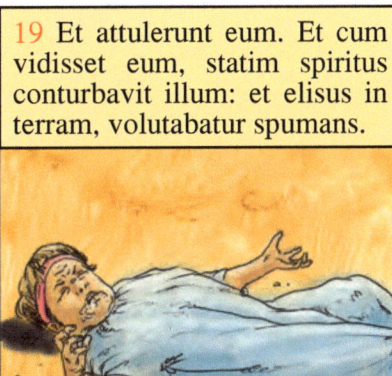

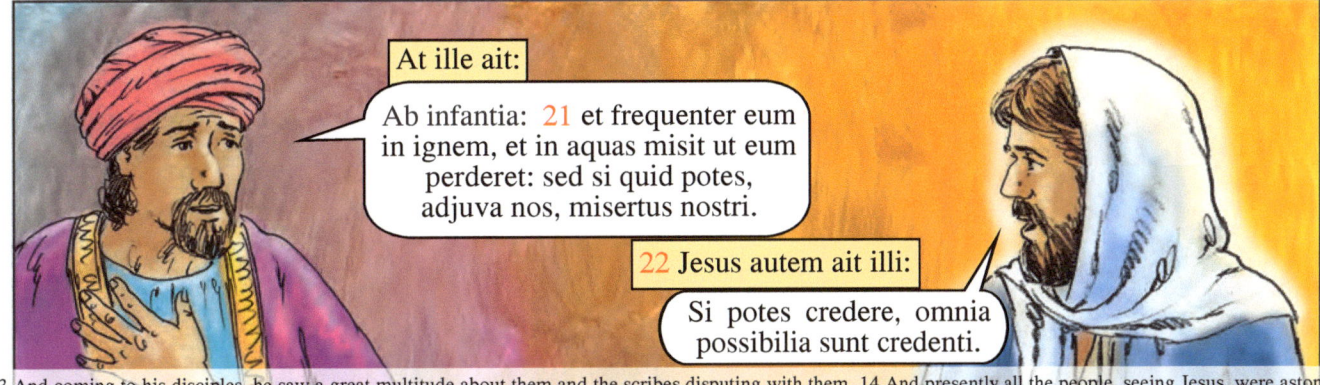

13 And coming to his disciples, he saw a great multitude about them and the scribes disputing with them. 14 And presently all the people, seeing Jesus, were astonished and struck with fear; and running to him, they were greeting him. 15 And he asked them, "What are you investigating among yourselves?" 16 And one from the multitude, answering back, said, "Master, I have brought my son to you, having a mute spirit; 17 which, wherever he takes him, bruises him and he foams and gnashes the teeth and languishes; and I spoke to your disciples to cast it out, and they were not able to." 18 Who, responding back to them, said, "O incredulous generation, how long will I be with you? How long will I endure you? Bring him to me!" 19 And they brought him. And when he had seen him, immediately the spirit troubled him and being thrown down upon the ground, he was rolling about foaming. 20 And he asked his father, "How long has this happened to him?" But he said, "From his infancy. 21 And oftentimes it casts him into the fire and into the waters to destroy him. But if you can do anything, help us, having compassion on us!" 22 And Jesus said to him, "If you are able to believe, all things are possible for the one believing."

Mark 9:23-32a

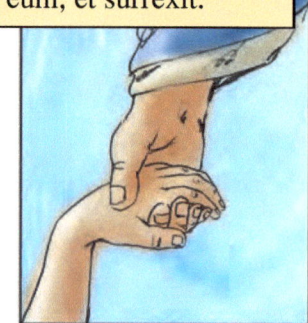

23 And incessantly the father of the boy was crying out said with tears, "I believe, Lord! Help my unbelief!" 24 And when Jesus saw the multitude running together, he was threatening the unclean spirit, saying to it, "Deaf and mute spirit, I command you, go out of him; and do not enter any more into him!" 25 And crying out and greatly tearing him, it went out of him. And he became as dead, so that many said this: "He is dead!" 26 But Jesus, taking him by the hand, lifted him up. And he arose. 27 And when he had entered into the house, his disciples secretly were asking him, "Why were we ourselves not able to cast it out?" 28 And he said to them, "This kind is not able to go out by anything, but by prayer and fasting." 29 And departing from there, they were passing through Galilee; and he was not wanting anyone to know. 30 Moreover, he was teaching his disciples and was saying to them this: "The Son of Humanity will be betrayed into the hands of men, and they will kill him; and after being killed, on the third day he will rise again." 31 But they were not understanding the saying; and they were being afraid to ask him. 32a And they came to Capernaum.

Mark 9:32b-43

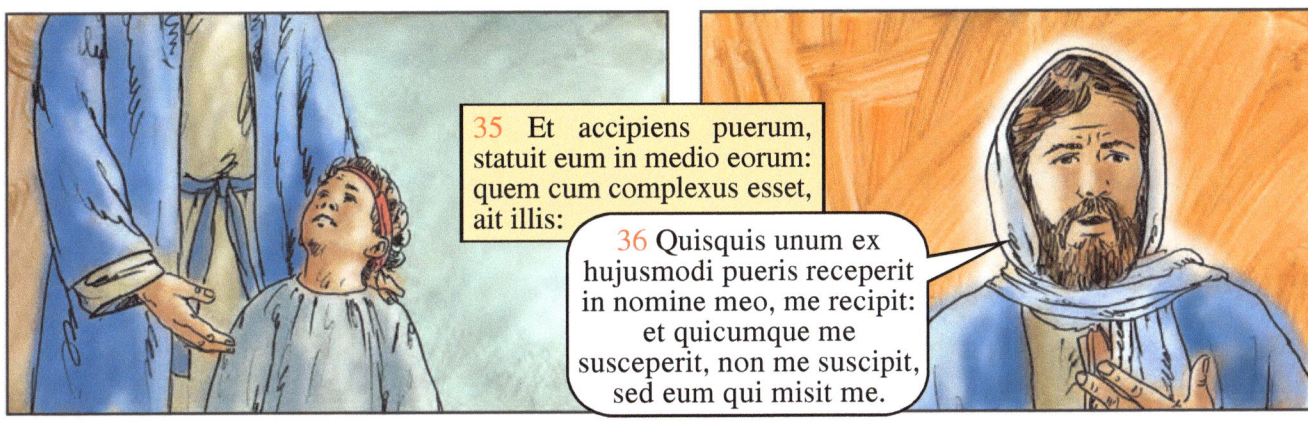

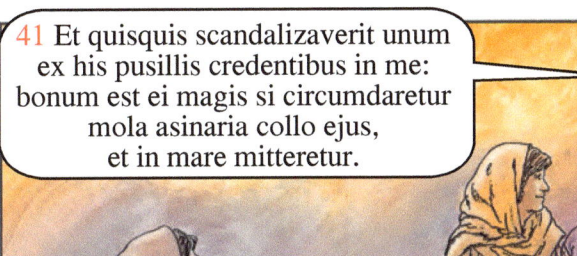

Qui cum domi essent, interrogabat eos: Quid in via tractabatis? 33 At illi tacebant: siquidem in via inter se disputaverunt: quis eorum major esset. 34 Et residens vocavit duodecim, et ait illis: Si quis vult primus esse, erit omnium novissimus, et omnium minister. 35 Et accipiens puerum, statuit eum in medio eorum: quem cum complexus esset, ait illis: 36 Quisquis unum ex hujusmodi pueris receperit in nomine meo, me recipit: et quicumque me susceperit, non me suscipit, sed eum qui misit me. 37 Respondit illi Joannes, dicens: Magister, vidimus quemdam in nomine tuo ejicientem dæmonia, qui non sequitur nos, et prohibuimus eum. 38 Jesus autem ait: Nolite prohibere eum: nemo est enim qui faciat virtutem in nomine meo, et possit cito male loqui de me: 39 qui enim non est adversum vos, pro vobis est. 40 Quisquis enim potum dederit vobis calicem aquæ in nomine meo, quia Christi estis: amen dico vobis, non perdet mercedem suam. 41 Et quisquis scandalizaverit unum ex his pusillis credentibus in me: bonum est ei magis si circumdaretur mola asinaria collo ejus, et in mare mitteretur. 42 Et si scandalizaverit te manus tua, abscide illam: bonum est tibi debilem introire in vitam, quam duas manus habentem ire in gehennam, in ignem inextinguibilem, 43 ubi vermis eorum non moritur, et ignis non extinguitur.

32b He, when they were in the house, was asking them, "What were you discussing on the way?" 33 But they were remaining quiet, for on the way they had disputed among themselves, which of them was the greatest. 34 And sitting down, he called the twelve and says to them, "If anyone desires to be first, he will be the last of all and servant of all." 35 And taking a child, he set him in the midst of them; whom when he had embraced, he said to them, 36 "Whosoever will receive one such child as this in my name receives me. And whosoever will receive me receives not me but him that sent me." 37 John answered him, saying, "Master, we saw someone casting out demons in your name, who is not following us; and we forbade him." 38 But Jesus said, "Do not forbid him!" For there is no one who does a miracle in my name and is able soon to speak badly about me. 39 For the one who is not against you is for you. 40 For whosoever will give you to drink a cup of water in my name, because you belong to Christ, Amen! I say to you, he will not lose his reward. 41 And whosoever will cause one of these little ones who believes in me to stumble, it would be better for this person that a millstone were hung about his neck and he were cast into the sea. 42 And if your hand causes you to stumble, cut it off; it is better for you to enter into life maimed, than having two hands to go into hell, into unquenchable fire, 43 where their worm does not die, and the fire is not extinguished.

Mark 9:44-10:4

Caput X

Mark 10:5-16

5 Quibus respondens Jesus, ait:

Ad duritiam cordis vestri scripsit vobis præceptum istud: 6 ab initio autem creaturæ masculum et feminam fecit eos Deus. 7 Propter hoc relinquet homo patrem suum et matrem, et adhærebit ad uxorem suam: 8 et erunt duo in carne una. Itaque jam non sunt duo, sed una caro. 9 Quod ergo Deus conjunxit, homo non separet.

10 Et in domo iterum discipuli ejus de eodem interrogaverunt eum. 11 Et ait illis:

Quicumque dimiserit uxorem suam, et aliam duxerit, adulterium committit super eam. 12 Et si uxor dimiserit virum suum, et alii nupserit, mœchatur.

13 Et offerebant illi parvulos ut tangeret illos. Discipuli autem comminabantur offerentibus. 14 Quos cum videret Jesus, indigne tulit, et ait illis:

Sinite parvulos venire ad me, et ne prohibueritis eos: talium enim est regnum Dei. 15 Amen dico vobis: Quisquis non receperit regnum Dei velut parvulus, non intrabit in illud.

16 Et complexans eos, et imponens manus super illos, benedicebat eos.

5 To whom Jesus, answering back, said, "Because of the hardness of your heart, he wrote you that precept; 6 however, from the beginning of the creation, 'God made them male and female. 7 For this reason, a man will leave his father and mother and will cleave to his wife. 8 And they two will be in one flesh.' Therefore, now they are not two, but one flesh. 9 Therefore, what God has joined together, let no person separate!" 10 And in the house again his disciples asked him concerning the same thing. 11 And he says to them, "Whosoever puts away his wife and marries another commits adultery against her. 12 And if the wife puts away her husband and is married to another, she commits adultery." 13 And they were bringing to him young children so that he would touch them. However, the disciples were rebuking them who were bringing (them). 14 Whom, when Jesus was seeing, he was much displeased and said to them, "Continue allowing the little children to come to me and do not forbid them! For, to such as these the kingdom of God belongs! 15 Amen! I say to you, whosoever will not receive the kingdom of God as a little child will not enter into it!" 16 And embracing them and laying his hands upon them, he was blessing them.

Mark 10:17-27

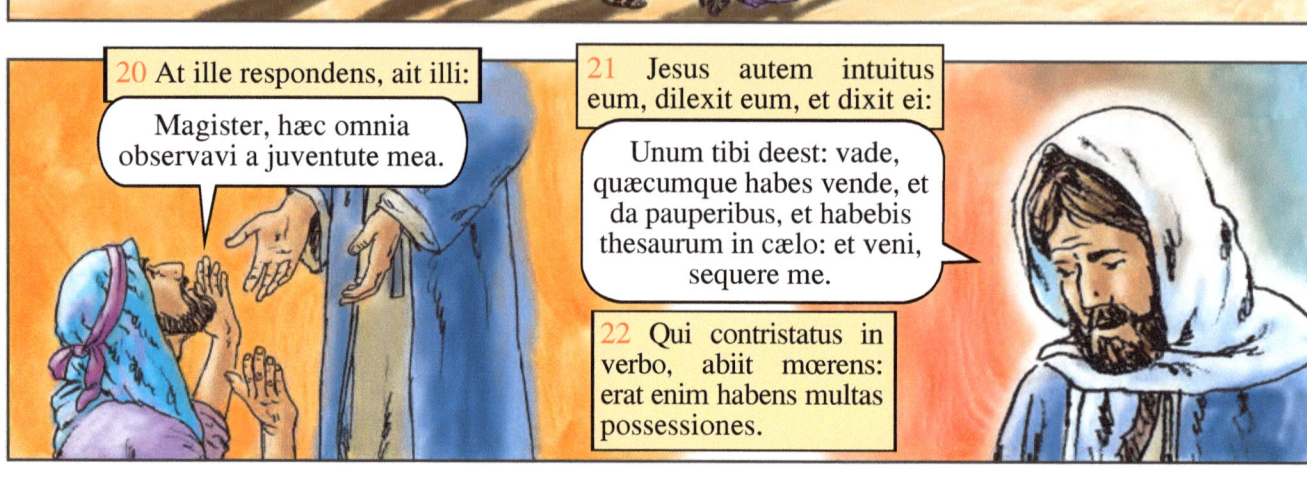
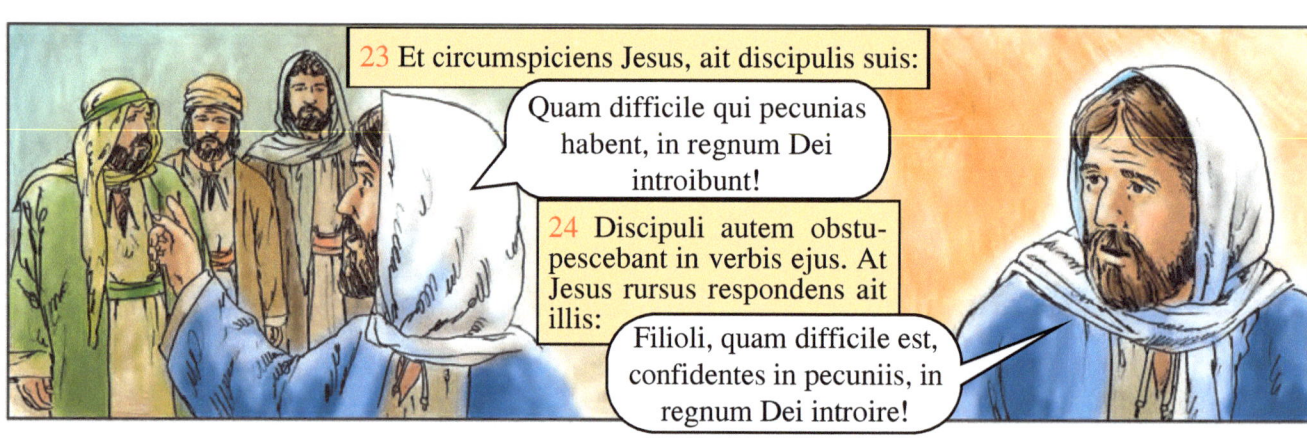

17 And when he had gone along on the way, a certain man, running up and kneeling before him, was asking him, "Good Master, what should I do so that I would receive everlasting life? 18 But Jesus said to him, "Why do you call me good? No one is good except God alone. 19 You know the commandments: 'Do not commit adultery, do not kill, do not steal, do not bear false witness, do not commit fraud, honor your father and mother.'" 20 But he, answering back, said to him, "Master, all these things I have observed from my youth." 21 However, Jesus, looking at him, loved him and said to him, "One thing is lacking for you. Go, sell whatsoever you have and give to the poor, and you will have treasure in heaven; and come, follow me." 22 Who, being struck sad at that saying, went away mourning; for he was having many possessions. 23 And Jesus, looking round about, says to his disciples, "How difficultly will they who have riches enter into the kingdom of God!" 24 Moreover, the disciples were astonished at his words. But Jesus, again answering back, says to them, "Little children, how hard it is for the ones trusting in riches to enter into the kingdom of God! 25 It is easier for a camel to pass through the eye of a needle than for a rich man to enter into the kingdom of God!" 26 Who were marveling more, saying to themselves, "Who even is able to be saved?!" 27 But Jesus, looking on them, says, "With humans it is impossible, but not with God; for all things are possible with God."

Mark 10:28-37

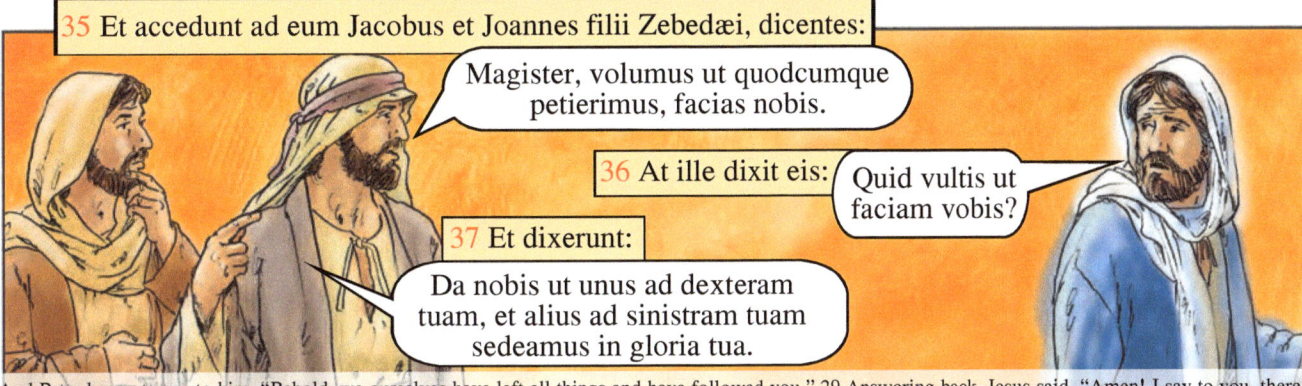

28 And Peter began to say to him, "Behold, we ourselves have left all things and have followed you." 29 Answering back, Jesus said, "Amen! I say to you, there is no one who has left house or brothers or sisters or father or mother or children or lands for my sake and for the gospel, 30 who will not receive a hundred times as much, now at this time; houses and brethren and sisters and mothers and children and lands, with persecutions; and in the future age, everlasting life. 31 But many who are first will be last, and the last first." 32 Now, they were on the way going up to Jerusalem; and Jesus was going before them, and they were astounded; and following (him) they were remaining afraid. And taking again the twelve, he began to tell which things were about to happen to him 33 (saying) this: "Behold! We are going up to Jerusalem, and the Son of Humanity will be betrayed to the chief priests and to the scribes and elders. And they will condemn him to death and will deliver him to the Gentiles; 34 and they will mock him and spit on him and scourge him and kill him; and on the third day he will rise again." 35 And James and John, the sons of Zebedee, come to him, saying, "Master, we want that whatsoever we will ask, you would do it for us." 36 But he said to them, "What do you want that I would do for you?" 37 And they said, "Grant to us that we may sit, one on your right hand and the other on your left hand, in your glory."

Mark 10:38-48

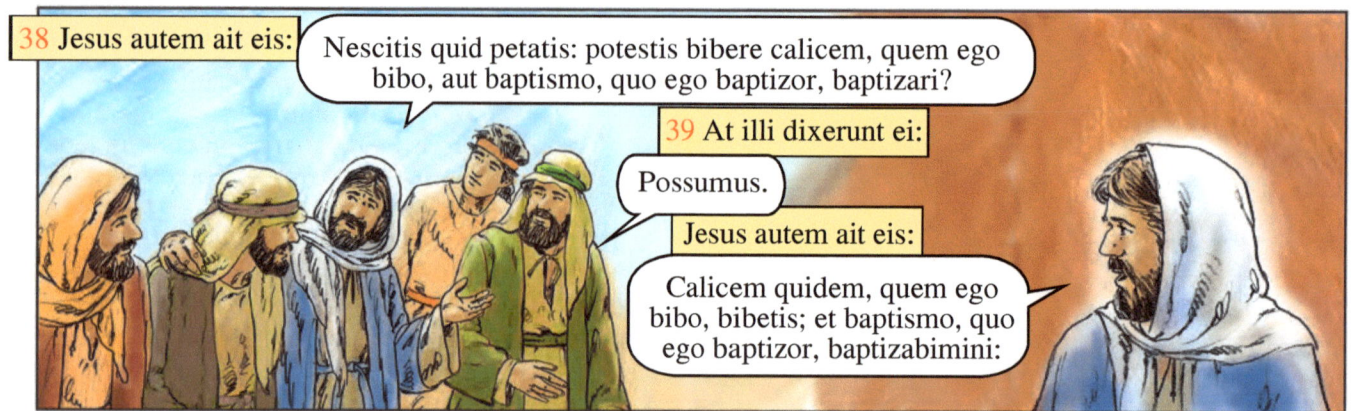

38 And Jesus said to them, "You do not know what you are asking! Are you able to drink of the cup that I myself drink of or be baptized with the baptism with which I myself am baptized?!" 39 But they said to him, "We are able!" But Jesus says to them, "You will indeed drink of the cup that I myself drink; and with the baptism with which I myself am baptized you will be baptized; 40 however, to sit on my right hand or on my left is not mine to give to you, but (is) for them for whom it is prepared." 41 And the ten, hearing it, began to be indignant at James and John. 42 But Jesus calling them, says to them, "You know that they who are seen to rule over the Gentiles dominate them; and their leaders have power over them. 43 But it is not thus among you, but whosoever wants to be greater will be your servant; 44 and whosoever will be first among you will be the servant of all. 45 For the Son of Humanity also did not come so that he is served, but so that he serves and gives his life a redemption for many." 46 And they came to Jericho; and as he went out of Jericho and his disciples and a very great multitude, Bartimeus, the blind man, the son of Timeus, was sitting next to the road begging. 47 Who, when he had heard that it was Jesus of Nazareth, began to cry out and to say, "Jesus, Son of David, have mercy on me!" 48 And many were rebuking him that he would be silent. But he was crying a great deal the more, "Son of David, have mercy on me!"

Mark 10:49-11:4

49 And Jesus, standing still, commanded him to be called. And they call the blind man, saying to him, "Be comforted! Arise, he calls you!" 50 Who, with garment cast off, leaped up and came to him. 51 And Jesus answering, said to him, "What do you want that I should do for you?" And the blind man said to him, "Rabboni, that I may see." 52 And responding, Jesus said to him, "Go! Your faith has made you whole." And immediately he saw and was following him on the road. 11:1 And when they were drawing near to Jerusalem and to Bethany at the mount of Olives, he sends two of his disciples, 2 and says to them, "Go into the village which is opposite you, and immediately entering it, you will find a young donkey tied upon on which no person has sat. Untie and bring it. 4 If anyone asks you, 'Why are you doing this?' say, 'The Lord needs him; and immediately he will send it back here.'" 4 And going their way, they found the young donkey tied before the gate outside at the crossroads; and they untied it.

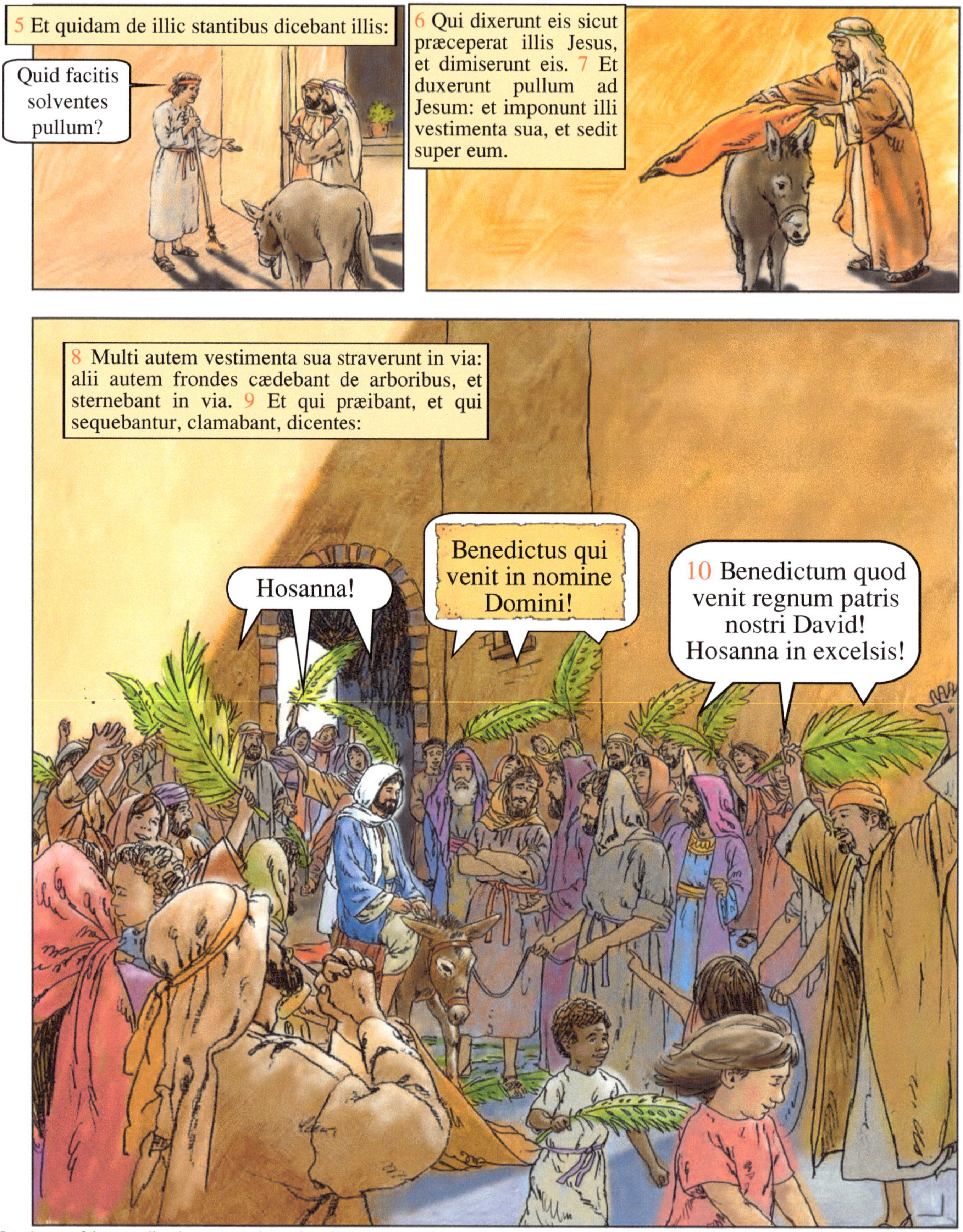

Mark 11:11-17

11 And he entered Jerusalem into the temple; and all things being looked at all around, when now the evening came, he went out to Bethany with the twelve. 12 And on the next day, when they came out from Bethany, he was hungry. 13 And when he had seen from afar a fig tree having leaves, he came, if perhaps he might find anything on it; and when he had come to it, he found nothing but leaves; for it was not the time for figs. 14 And responding, he said to it, "No longer may anyone eat fruit from you forever!" And his disciples were hearing it. 15 And they came to Jerusalem. And when he had entered into the temple, he began to cast out the ones selling and buying in the temple; and he over threw the tables of the moneychangers and the chairs of the ones selling doves; 16 and he was not allowing that anyone should carry a vessel through the temple. 17 And he was teaching, saying to them, "Is it not written this: 'My house will be called the house of prayer to all nations,' but you have made 'it a den of thieves.'"

Mark 11:18-27

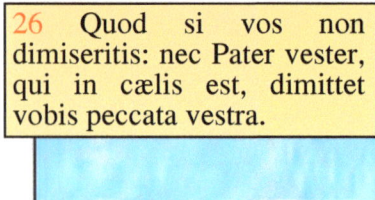

18 Which being heard, the chief priests and the scribes were seeking how they might destroy him; for they were fearing him, because the whole multitude was admiring about his teaching. 19 And when evening had come, he was going out of the city. 20 And when they were passing by in the morning, they saw the fig tree dried up from the roots. 21 And remembering, Peter said to him, "Rabbi, behold the fig tree which you cursed is withered away!" 22 And answering back, Jesus says to them, "Have the faith of God! 23 Amen! I am saying to you that whosoever will say to this mountain, 'Be removed and be cast into the sea,' and will not stagger in his heart, but believe that whatsoever he will say, is done, it is done for him. 24 Therefore, I say to you, all things, whatsoever praying you ask, believe that you will receive, and they will come to you. 25 And when you will stand to pray, forgive if you have anything against anyone; so that your Father also, who is in heaven, may forgive you your sins. 26 But if you will not forgive, neither will your Father who is in heaven forgive you your sins." 27 And they come again to Jerusalem. And when he was walking in the temple, there come to him the chief priests and the scribes and the elders;

28 and they say to him, "By what authority are you doing these things? And who has given you this authority so that you would do these things?" 29 However, Jesus, answering back, said to them, "I will also ask you one word and respond back to me; and I will tell you by what authority I do these things. 30 The baptism of John, was it from heaven or from humans? Respond to me!" 31 But they were thinking to themselves, saying, "If we say, 'From heaven'; he will say, 'Why then did you not believe him?' 32 If we say, 'From humans', we fear the people." For all men were holding John that he was truly a prophet. 33 And answering back, they say to Jesus, "We do not know." And answering back, Jesus says to them, "Neither do I myself tell you by what authority I am doing these things." 12:1 And he began to speak to them in parables: "A certain person planted a vineyard and made a hedge about it and dug a place for the wine vat and built a tower and contracted it to farmers, and he departed abroad. 2 And he sent a servant to the farmers in time to receive from the farmers the fruit of the vineyard.

Mark 12:3-16a

3 Qui apprehensum eum ceciderunt, et dimiserunt vacuum.

4 Et iterum misit ad illos alium servum: et illum in capite vulneraverunt, et contumeliis affecerunt. 5 Et rursum alium misit,

et illum occiderunt:

et plures alios: quosdam cædentes, alios vero occidentes. 6 Adhuc ergo unum habens filium carissimum, et illum misit ad eos novissimum, dicens:

"Quia reverebuntur filium meum."

7 Coloni autem dixerunt ad invicem:

"Hic est hæres: venite, occidamus eum: et nostra erit hæreditas."

8 Et apprehendentes eum, occiderunt: et ejecerunt extra vineam.

9 Quid ergo faciet dominus vineæ? Veniet, et perdet colonos, et dabit vineam aliis. 10 Nec scripturam hanc legistis:

Lapidem quem reprobaverunt ædificantes, hic factus est in caput anguli: 11 a Domino factum est istud, et est mirabile in oculis nostris?

12 Et quærebant eum tenere: et timuerunt turbam: cognoverunt enim quoniam ad eos parabolam hanc dixerit. Et relicto eo abierunt.

13 Et mittunt ad eum quosdam ex pharisæis, et herodianis, ut eum caperent in verbo. 14 Qui venientes dicunt ei:

"Magister, scimus quia verax es, et non curas quemquam: nec enim vides in faciem hominum, sed in veritate viam Dei doces. Licet dari tributum Cæsari, an non dabimus?"

15 Qui sciens versutiam illorum, ait illos:

"Quid me tentatis? afferte mihi denarium ut videam."

16 At illi attulerunt ei. Et ait illis:

"Cujus est imago hæc, et inscriptio?"

3 Who, having laid hands on him, beat and sent him away empty. 4 And again he sent to them another servant; and him they wounded in the head and afflicted him insultingly. 5 And again he sent another, and him they killed; and many others, of whom some they beat, and others they killed. 6 Therefore, having yet one most dear son, he also sent him to them last of all, saying this: 'They will respect my son.' 7 But the farmers said one to another, 'This is the heir; come, let us kill him; and the inheritance will be ours!' 8 And laying hold of him, they killed him; and cast him out of the vineyard. 9 What, therefore, will the lord of the vineyard do? He will come, and destroy those farmers, and will give the vineyard to others. 10 And have you not read this Scripture, 'The stone which the builders rejected, the same is made the head of the corner; 11 by the Lord has this been done, and it is wonderful in our eyes!'" 12 And they were seeking to lay hands on him; but they feared the crowd; for they knew that he spoke this parable to them. And with him remaining, they departed. 13 And they sent to him some of the Pharisees, and of the Herodians, so that they would catch him in a word. 14 Who coming, say to him, "Master, we know that you are a true speaker and care not for anyone; for you regard not the person of humans, but teach the way of God in truth. Is it lawful to give tribute to Caesar? Or will we not give it?" 15 Who knowing their craftiness, said to them, "Why are you tempting me? Bring me a denarius that I may see it." 16a And they brought it him. And he says to them, "Whose is this image and inscription?"

Mark 12:16b-30

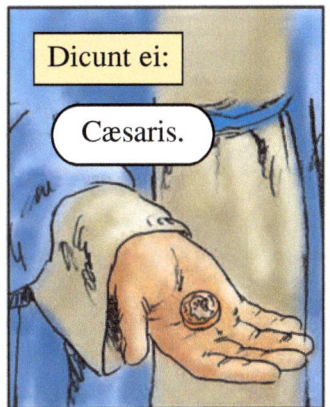

16b They say to him, "Caesar's." 17 However, answering back, Jesus said to them, "Render therefore to Caesar the things that are Caesar's and to God the things that are God's." And they were marveling over him. 18 And there came to him the Sadducees, who say there is no resurrection; and they were asking him, saying, 19 "Master, Moses wrote to us that if any man's brother dies and leaves a wife and leaves behind no children, his brother should take his wife and raise up seed for his brother. 20 Now there were seven brethren; and the first took the wife and died with no seed left behind. 21 And the second took her and died; and neither did he leave behind any seed. And the third in like manner. 22 And similarly all seven took her; and they did not leave seed. Last of all the woman also was deceased. 23 In the resurrection, therefore, when they will rise again, whose wife of them will she be? For seven had her as a wife." 24 And answering back, Jesus said to them, "Are you not for this reason mistaken, because you do not know the Scriptures nor the power of God? (Yes!) 25 For when they will rise again from the dead, they will neither marry, nor be married, but they are just like the angels in heaven. 26 Moreover, concerning the dead that they rise again, have you not read in the book of Moses, how in the bush God spoke to him, saying, 'I am the God of Abraham and the God of Isaac and the God of Jacob'? 27 He is not the God of the dead, but of the living. You yourselves, therefore, do greatly err!" 28 And there came one of the scribes who had heard them reasoning together, and seeing that he had responded back to them well, asked him which was the first commandment of all. 29 However, Jesus answered back to him this: "The first commandment of all is, 'Hear, O Israel, the Lord your God is one God. 30 And you shall love the Lord your God with your whole heart and with your whole soul and with your whole mind and with your whole strength.' This is the first commandment.

Mark 12:31-40

31 Moreover, the second is like it: 'You shall love your neighbor as yourself.' There is no other commandment greater than these." 32 And the scribe said to him, "Well, Master, you have spoken in truth that there is one God and there is no other besides him. 33 And that he should be loved with the whole heart and with the whole understanding and with the whole soul and with the whole strength. And to love one's neighbor as one's self is greater than all burnt offerings and sacrifices." 34 And Jesus seeing that he had answered wisely, said to him, "You are not far from the kingdom of God." And no one after that was daring to ask him any question. 35 And responding back, Jesus was saying (while) teaching in the temple, "How do the scribes say that Christ is the son of David? 36 For David himself says by the Holy Spirit, 'The Lord said to my Lord, "Sit on my right hand, until I make your enemies your footstool."' 37 David, therefore, himself calls him 'Lord,' and whence is he his son?!" And a great multitude heard him gladly. 38 And he was saying to them in his teaching, "Beware of the scribes, who love to walk in long robes and to be saluted in the marketplace, 39 and to sit in the first chairs in the synagogues and to have the highest places at suppers; 40 who devour the houses of widows under the pretense of long prayer. These will receive greater judgment."

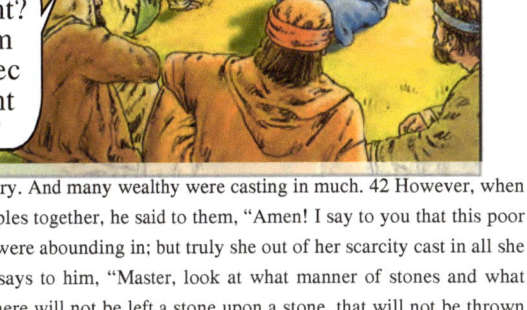

Mark 13:5-20

5 Et respondens Jesus cœpit dicere illis: Videte ne quid vos seducat: 6 multi enim venient in nomine meo, dicentes quia ego sum: et multos seducent. 7 Cum audieritis autem bella, et opiniones bellorum, ne timueritis: oportet enim hæc fieri: sed nondum finis. 8 Exsurget enim gens contra gentem, et regnum super regnum, et erunt terræmotus per loca, et fames. Initium dolorum hæc. 9 Videte autem vosmetipsos. Tradent enim vos in consiliis, et in synagogis vapulabitis, et ante præsides et reges stabitis propter me, in testimonium illis. 10 Et in omnes gentes primum oportet prædicari Evangelium. 11 Et cum duxerint vos tradentes, nolite præcogitare quid loquamini: sed quod datum vobis fuerit in illa hora, id loquimini: non enim vos estis loquentes, sed Spiritus Sanctus. 12 Tradet autem frater fratrem in mortem, et pater filium: et consurgent filii in parentes, et morte afficient eos. 13 Et eritis odio omnibus propter nomen meum. Qui autem sustinuerit in finem, hic salvus erit. 14 Cum autem videritis abominationem desolationis stantem, ubi non debet, qui legit, intelligat: tunc qui in Judæa sunt, fugiant in montes: 15 et qui super tectum, ne descendat in domum, nec introëat ut tollat quid de domo sua: 16 et qui in agro erit, non revertatur retro tollere vestimentum suum. 17 Væ autem prægnantibus et nutrientibus in illis diebus. 18 Orate vero ut hieme non fiant. 19 Erunt enim dies illi tribulationes tales quales non fuerunt ab initio creaturæ, quam condidit Deus usque nunc, neque fient. 20 Et nisi breviasset Dominus dies, non fuisset salva omnis caro: sed propter electos, quos elegit, breviavit dies.

5 And answering back, Jesus began to say to them, "Take heed lest anyone deceive you." 6 For many will come in my name saying this: 'I am he'; and they will deceive many. 7 Moreover, when you will hear of wars and rumors of wars, fear not. For such things are necessary to happen; but the end is not yet. 8 For nation will rise against nation and kingdom against kingdom, and there will be earthquakes in diverse places and famines. These things are the beginning of sorrows. 9 But look to yourselves. For they will deliver you up to councils, and in the synagogues you will be beaten, and you will stand before governors and kings for my sake, for a testimony to them. 10 And to all nations the gospel must first be preached. 11 And when they will lead you and deliver you up, be not thoughtful beforehand what you will speak; but whatsoever will be given you in that hour, speak that; for it is not you who is speaking, but the Holy Spirit. 12 And the brother will betray his brother to death, and the father his son; and children will rise up against their parents and will cause their death. 13 And you will be hated by all people for my name's sake. But he who will endure to the end, this one will be saved. 14 And when you will see the abomination of desolation, standing where it ought not be (let the one reading understand), then the ones who are in Judea should flee to the mountains; 15 and let him who is on the housetop not go down into the house nor enter within to take anything out of his house; 16 and let him who will be in the field not turn back to take up his garment. 17 Moreover, woe to them that are with child and nursing in those days! 18 Pray truly that these things do not happen in winter! 19 For in those days will be tribulations of such a kind as were not from the beginning of the creation which God created until now, nor will there be. 20 And unless the Lord had shortened the days, no flesh would have been saved; but, for the sake of the elect whom he has chosen, he has shortened the days.

21 And then if anyone will say to you, "Look, here is Christ! Look, there!' do not believe. 22 For false Christs and false prophets will rise up, and they will show signs and wonders, to seduce, if it were possible, even the elect. 23 Take heed, therefore; behold, I foretold all things to you. 24 But in those days, after that tribulation, the sun will be darkened and the moon will not give its light; 25 and the stars of heaven will be falling down and the powers that are in heaven will be moved. 26 And then will they see the Son of Humanity coming in the clouds with great power and glory. 27 And then he will send his angels and will gather together his elect from the four winds, from the uttermost part of the earth to the uttermost part of heaven. 28 Now from the fig tree learn a parable. When its branch is now tender and the leaves are come forth, you know that summer is very near. 29 So you also, when you will see these things come to pass, know that it is very near, even at the doors. 30 Amen! I say to you that this generation will not pass until all these things happen. 31 Heaven and earth will pass away, but my word will not pass away. 32 But of that day or hour no one knows, neither the angels in heaven, nor the Son, except the Father. 33 Take heed, watch, and pray; for you do not know when the time is. 34 It is just like a person who, going into a far country, left his house and gave authority to his servants over every work and commanded the doorkeeper to watch. 35 Watch, therefore (for you know not when the lord of the house comes, late, or at midnight, or at the cock crowing, or in the morning), 36 lest, when he comes suddenly, he finds you sleeping. 37 Moreover, what I saying to you, I am saying to all: Be watching!"

Mark 14:1-9

14:1 It was now two days before the feast of the Passover and the unleavened bread, and the chief priests and the scribes were seeking how they might seize him by deception, and slay him. 2 For they were saying, "Not during the feast, lest perhaps there would be a riot among the people." 3 And while he was at Bethany in the house of Simon the leper, and was sitting at the table, a woman came having an alabaster jar of ointment of pure nard—very costly. And with the jar being broken, she poured it over his head. 4 But there were some who were indignant among themselves, and saying, "What has she done with this wasted ointment?! 5 For this might have been sold for more than three hundred denarii, and given to the poor." So, they were grumbling against her. 6 But Jesus said, "Leave her alone! Why do you trouble her? She has done a good work for me. 7 For you always have the poor with you, and whenever you want to, you are to do them good; but you will not always have me. 8 She has done what she could. She has prepared to anoint my body for the burying. 9 Most certainly, I tell you, wherever this Good News may be preached throughout the whole world, that which this woman has done will also be spoken for her memorial."

Mark 14:10-18

10 And Judas Iscariot, one of the twelve, went away to the chief priests, in order that he would deliver him to them. 11 They, when they heard it, were glad, and promised that they would give him money. And he was seeking how he might conveniently deliver him. 12 And on the first day of unleavened bread, when they were sacrificing the Passover, his disciples asked him, "Where do you want us to go and prepare for you to eat the Passover?" 13 And he sent two of his disciples, and said to them, "Go into the city, and there you will meet a person carrying a pitcher of water. Follow him, 14 and wherever he enters in, tell the master of the house what the Teacher says, 'Where is the guest room, where I may eat the Passover with my disciples?' 15 And he will himself show you a large upper room, laid out. Prepare for us there." 16 And his disciples went out, and came into the city, and found things as he had said to them, and they prepared the Passover. 17 Moreover, when it became evening, he came with the twelve. 18 And as they sat and were eating, Jesus said, "Most certainly I tell you, that one of you will betray me—he who eats with me."

Mark 14:19-29

19 At illi cœperunt contristari, et dicere ei singulatim:

Numquid ego?

20 Qui ait illis:

Unus ex duodecim, qui intingit mecum manum in catino.

21 Et Filius quidem hominis vadit sicut scriptum est de eo: væ autem homini illi per quem Filius hominis tradetur! bonum erat ei, si non esset natus homo ille.

22 Et manducantibus illis, accepit Jesus panem: et benedicens fregit, et dedit eis,

et ait:

Sumite, hoc est corpus meum.

23 Et accepto calice, gratias agens dedit eis: et biberunt ex illo omnes. 24 Et ait illis:

Hic est sanguis meus novi testamenti, qui pro multis effundetur. 25 Amen dico vobis, quia jam non bibam de hoc genimine vitis usque in diem illum, cum illud bibam novum in regno Dei.

26 Et hymno dicto exierunt in montem Olivarum. 27 Et ait eis Jesus:

Omnes scandalizabimini in me in nocte ista: quia scriptum est:

Percutiam pastorem, et dispergentur oves.

28 Sed postquam resurrexero, præcedam vos in Galilæam.

29 Petrus autem ait illi:

Et si omnes scandalizati fuerint in te, sed non ego.

19 But they began to be sorrowful, and to ask him one by one, "Surely not I?" 20 He said to them, "It is one of the twelve, he who dips with me in the dish. 21 For the Son of Humanity goes just as it is written about him, but woe to that person by whom the Son of Humanity is betrayed! It would be better for that person if he had not been born!" 22 And as they were eating, Jesus took bread, and blessing it he broke it, and gave to them, and said, "Take, eat. This is my body." 23 And having taken the cup, giving thanks, he gave it to them and they all drank from it. 24 And he said to them, "This is my blood of the new covenant, which is poured out for many. 25 Most certainly I tell you, I will no more drink of the fruit of the vine, until that day when I drink it anew in God's Kingdom." 26 And with a hymn being sung, they went out to the Mount of Olives. 27 And Jesus says to them, "All of you will be made to stumble with regard to me in this night, for it is written, 'I will strike the shepherd, and the sheep will be scattered.' 28 However, after I will arise, I will go before you into Galilee." 29 But Peter said to him, "Even if all will stumble with regard to you, yet I will not."

Mark 14:30-37

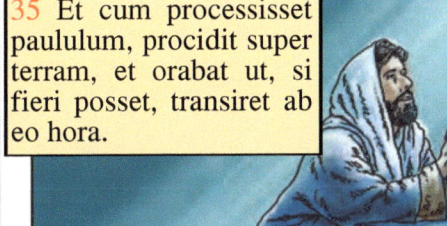

30 Jesus says to him, "Most certainly I tell you, that you today in this night, before the rooster crows twice, three times you will deny me." 31 But he was speaking all the more, "Even if I must die at the same time together with you, I will not deny you." Moreover, they all also were speaking similarly. 32 And they went to a place whose name was Gethsemane. And he says to his disciples, "Sit here, while I pray." 33 And he takes with him Peter, James, and John, and began to be struck with fear and distressed. 34 And he says to them, "My soul is exceedingly sorrowful to death. Stay here, and watch." 35 And when he had gone forward a little, he fell on the ground and was praying that, if it were possible, the hour would pass away from him. 36 And he said, "Abba, Father, all things are possible to you. Please remove this cup from me. However, not what I want, but what you want." 37 And he comes and finds them sleeping, and says to Peter, "Simon, are you sleeping? Couldn't you watch one hour?"

Mark 14:38-47

38 Watch and pray, so that you would not enter into temptation. The spirit indeed is willing; the flesh however is weak." 39 And again leaving, he prayed, saying the same words. 40 And returning, he again found them sleeping (for their eyes were very heavy) and they were not knowing how to answer him. 41 And he came the third time, and says to them, "Sleep on now, and rest. It is enough. The hour has come. Behold, the Son of Humanity will be betrayed into the hands of sinners. 42 Arise! Let's get going. Behold, the one who betrays me is near." 43 And, while he was still speaking, Judas, one of the twelve, came and with him a multitude with swords and clubs, from the chief priests, the scribes, and the elders. 44 Moreover, he who betrayed him had given them a sign, saying, "Whomever I will kiss, that is he. Seize him, and lead him away cautiously." 45 An when he had come, immediately approaching him he says, "Greetings, Rabbi!" and kissed him. 46 But they laid their hands on him and seized him. 47 But someone of those who stood by, drawing his sword, struck the servant of the high priest, and cut off his ear.

Mark 14:48-59

48 And Jesus responding, said to them, "Just as against a robber have you come out with swords and clubs to seize me? 49 Daily I was with you in the temple teaching, and you didn't arrest me. But this [is occurring] so that the Scriptures are fulfilled." 50 Then, his disciples abandoning him, all fled. 51 However, a certain young man was following him, wrapped with a linen cloth around his naked body; and they grabbed him, 52 but he, with linen thrown off, fled from them naked. 53 And they led Jesus away to the high priest; and all the chief priests, the elders, and the scribes were convened. 54 Peter however had followed him from a distance, until he came into the court of the high priest; and he was sitting with the officers at the fire, and was warming himself. 55 Indeed, the chief priests and the whole council were seeking witnesses against Jesus to put him to death; and they were not finding any. 56 For many were speaking false testimony against him, and their testimony didn't agree with each other. 57 And some rising up were offering false testimony against him, saying this: 58 "We ourselves heard him saying, 'I myself will destroy this temple made with hands, and in three days I will build another made without hands.'" 59 And their testimony was not consistent.

Mark 14:60-69

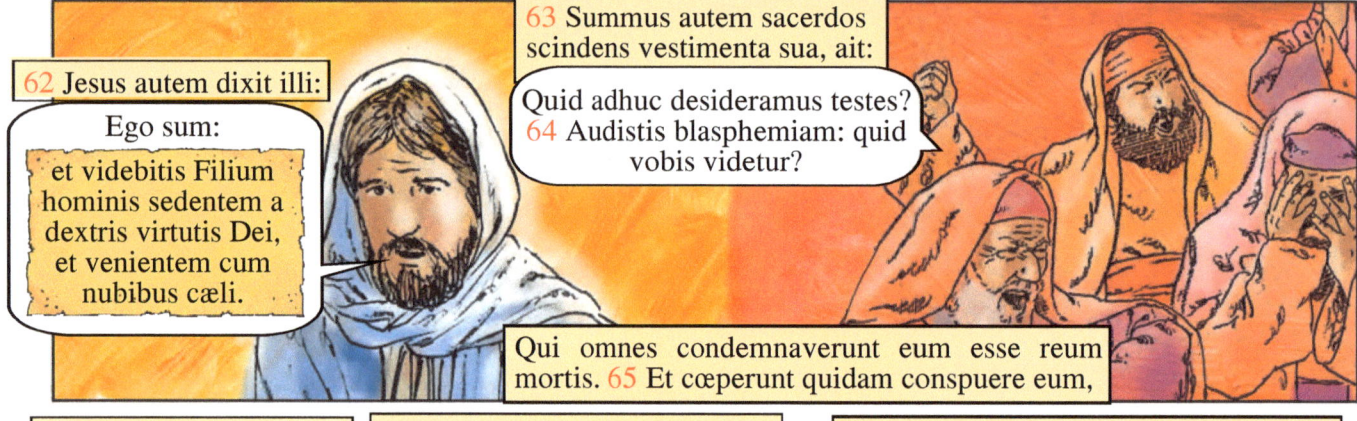

60 And the high priest, standing in the middle, asked Jesus saying, "Don't you offer some answer against that which is being testified against you by these men?" 61 But he was remaining quiet, and answered nothing. In return, the high priest was asking him, "Are you yourself the Christ, the Son of the blessed God?" 62 So Jesus said to him, "I myself am; and you will see the Son of Humanity sitting at the right hand of the power of God, and coming with the clouds of heaven." 63 Next, the high priest tore his clothes, and says, "Why are still needing witnesses? 64 You have heard the blasphemy! What does it appear to you?" They all condemned him to be worthy of death. 65 And some began to spit on him, and to cover his face, and to beat him with fists, and to say to him, "Prophesy!" And the officers were striking him with the palms of their hands. 66 And when Peter was in the courtyard below, one of the maids of the high priest comes, 67 and when she saw Peter warming himself, she, looking at him, says, "You also were with Jesus the Nazarene!" 68 But he denied it, saying, "I neither know, nor understand what you are saying." And he went out on the porch, and the rooster crowed. 69 However, in turn when the maid saw him, she began to say to those around this: "This is one of them."

Mark 14:70-15:8

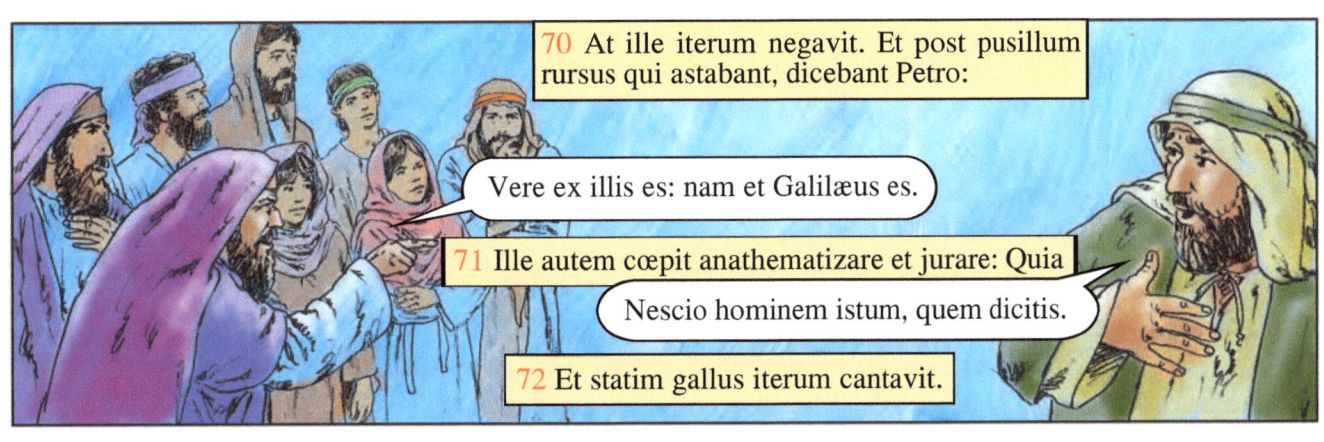

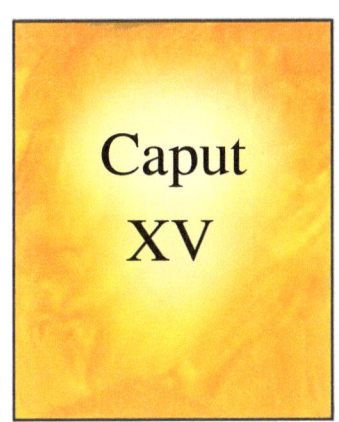

70 But he again denied it. And after a little while in turn those who were standing by were saying to Peter, "Truly you are one of them, for you are also a Galilean." 71 But he began to curse, and to swear this: "I don't know this person of whom you are speaking!" 72 And immediately the rooster crowed the second time. And Peter remembered the word that Jesus had spoken to him, "Before the rooster crows twice, three times you will deny me." And he began to weep. 15:1 And straightway in the morning, the chief priests holding a consultation with the elders and the scribes and the whole council, binding Jesus, led him away, and delivered (him) to Pilate. 2 And Pilate asked him, "Are you yourself the king of the Jews?" But he answering back, says to him, "You say it." 3 And the chief priests were accusing him in many ways. 4 Moreover, Pilate again asked him, saying, "Don't you answer anything? See in how many ways they are accusing you!" 5 But Jesus still answered nothing, so that thus Pilate was marveling. 6 Now on the festival day he was wanting to release to them one of the prisoners, whomsoever they had demanded. 7 Moreover, there was one whom they were calling Barabbas, who was put in prison with some seditious men, who in the sedition had committed murder. 8 And when the multitude had come up, they began to ask just as he always was doing for them.

9 But Pilate answered back to them, and said, "Do you want that I release to you 'The King of the Jews'?" 10 For he was knowing that the chief priests had delivered him up out of envy. 11 But the chief priests moved the people, so that he would rather release Barabbas to them. 12 However, Pilate again answering back, says to them, "What, therefore, do you want that I do to 'The King of the Jews'?" 13 But they again cried out, "Crucify him!" 14 However, Pilate was saying to them, "What evil, in fact, did he do?" But they were crying out the more, "Crucify him!" 15 And so Pilate, wanting to satisfy the people, released to them Barabbas, and delivered up Jesus having been cut up with whips, so that he was crucified. 16 Moreover, the soldiers led him away into the court of the palace, and they called together the whole band. 17 And they cloth him with purple, and, braiding a crown of thorns, they place it upon him. 18 And they began to salute him, "Hail, King of the Jews!" 19 And they were striking his head with a reed; and they were spitting on him, and bowing their knees, they were "honoring" him. 20 And after they had mocked him, they took off the purple from him, and put his own garments on him; and they led him out so that they would crucify him. 21 And they forced someone passing by, Simon a Cyrenian, coming from the country, the father of Alexander and of Rufus, so that he was taking up his cross.

Mark 15:22-24a

22 Et perducunt illum in Golgotha locum: quod est interpretatum Calvariæ locus.

23 Et dabant ei bibere myrrhatum vinum: et non accepit. 24 Et crucifigentes eum,

22 And they bring him into the place called Golgotha, which being interpreted is, "The place of the Skull." 23 And they were giving him to drink wine mingled with myrrh; and he did not accept it. 24a And crucifying him,

Mark 15:24b-28

diviserunt vestimenta ejus, mittentes sortem super eis, quis quid tolleret.

25 Erat autem hora tertia: et crucifixerunt eum. 26 Et erat titulus causæ ejus inscriptus:

Rex Judæorum.

27 Et cum eo crucifigunt duos latrones: unum a dextris, et alium a sinistris ejus. 28 Et impleta est Scriptura, quæ dicit: Et cum iniquis reputatus est.

24b they divided his garments, casting lots for them, who would take what. 25 Now it was the third hour; and they crucified him. 26 And the inscription of his accusation was inscribed, "The King of the Jews." 27 And with him they crucify two brigands; the one on his right hand, and the other on his left. 28 And the Scripture was fulfilled, which says, "And with the wicked he was reckoned."

Mark 15:29-40a

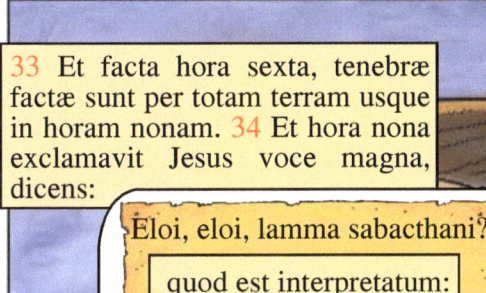

29 And ones passing by were blaspheming him, shaking their heads and saying, "Vah, you who destroy the temple of God and in three days build it up again! 30 Save yourself, coming down from the cross!" 31 In like manner also the chief priests, mocking, were saying with the scribes to one another, "He saved others; himself he is not able to save! 32 Let Christ, the king of Israel, come down now from the cross, so that we may see and believe." And the ones who were crucified with him were reviling him. 33 And when the sixth hour came, darkness was over the whole earth until the ninth hour. 34 And at the ninth hour, Jesus cried out with a loud voice, saying, "Eloi, Eloi, lamma sabacthani?" Which is, being interpreted, "My God, My God, why have you forsaken me?" 35 And some of the bystanders, hearing, were saying, "Behold, he calls Elijah." 36 Moreover, one running and filling a sponge with vinegar and putting it upon a reed, was giving him to drink, saying, "Stay, let us see if Elijah comes to take him down." 37 However, Jesus, having cried out with a loud voice, expired. 38 And the veil of the temple was rent in two, from the top to the bottom. 39 Moreover, the centurion seeing, who was standing opposite him, in what manner crying out he expired, said, "Truly, this person was the son of God!" 40a Now there were also women looking from afar,

Mark 15:40b-16:4

inter quas erat Maria Magdalene, et Maria Jacobi minoris, et Joseph mater, et Salome: 41 et cum esset in Galilæa, sequebantur eum, et ministrabant ei, et aliæ multæ, quæ simul cum eo ascenderant Jerosolymam.

42 Et cum jam sero esset factum (quia erat parasceve, quod est ante sabbatum), 43 43 venit Joseph ab Arimathæa nobilis decurio, qui et ipse erat exspectans regnum Dei, et audacter introivit ad Pilatum, et petiit corpus Jesu.

44 Pilatus autem mirabatur si jam obiisset. Et accersito centurione, interrogavit eum si jam mortuus esset. 45 Et cum cognovisset a centurione, donavit corpus Joseph. 46 Joseph autem mercatus sindonem, et deponens eum involvit sindone, et posuit eum in monumento quod erat excisum de petra,

et advolvit lapidem ad ostium monumenti. 47 Maria autem Magdalene et Maria Joseph aspiciebant ubi poneretur.

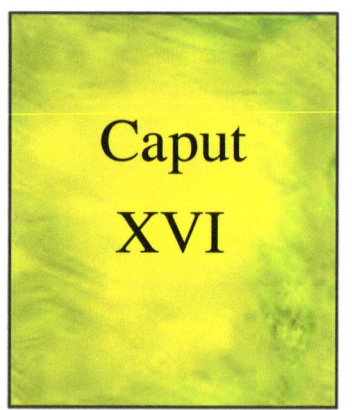

Caput XVI

1 Et cum transisset sabbatum, Maria Magdalene, et Maria Jacobi, et Salome emerunt aromata ut venientes ungerent Jesum. 2 Et valde mane una sabbatorum, veniunt ad monumentum, orto jam sole. 3 Et dicebant ad invicem:

Quis revolvet nobis lapidem ab ostio monumenti?

4 Et respicientes viderunt revolutum lapidem. Erat quippe magnus valde.

40b among whom was Mary Magdalene and Mary, the mother of James the Lesser, and the mother of Joseph, and Salome; 41 and, when he was in Galilee, these women were following him and were ministering to him, and many other women who likewise had come up with him to Jerusalem. 42 And when evening had now come (because it was the eve of Passover, that is, the day before the Sabbath), 43 Joseph of Arimathea, a noble councilman, who also himself was looking for the kingdom of God, came and boldly entered to Pilate and asked for the body of Jesus. 44 However, Pilate was wondering whether he had already died. And with the centurion summoned, he asked him if he were already dead. 45 And when he had learned from the centurion, he gave the body to Joseph. 46 Then Joseph, buying fine linen and taking him down, wrapped him up in the fine linen and laid him in a tomb which was hewn out of a rock, and he rolled a stone to the entrance of the tomb. 47 And Mary Magdalene and Mary the mother of Joseph, were watching where he was laid. 16:1 And when the Sabbath had past, Mary Magdalene and Mary the mother of James and Salome bought spices so that coming they would anoint Jesus. 2 And very early on the first day of the week, they come to the tomb with the sun now risen. 3 And they were saying to one another, "Who will roll back for us the stone from the entrance of the tomb?" 4 And looking, they saw the stone rolled back. For it was very large.

Mark 16:5-13

5 And entering into the tomb, they saw a young man sitting on the right side, clothed with a white robe; and they were astonished. 6 Who says to them, "Do not be terrified! You are seeking Jesus of Nazareth, who was crucified. He is risen, he is not here; behold the place where they laid him! 7 But go, tell his disciples, and Peter, that he goes before you into Galilee. There you will see him just as he told you." 8 However, they going out, fled from the tomb; for a trembling and fear had seized them; and they said nothing to anyone; for they were remaining afraid. 9 But he rising early the first day of the week, appeared first to Mary Magdalene from whom he had cast seven demons. 10 She, going, reported to those who had been with him who were mourning and weeping. 11 And they, hearing that he was living and had been seen by her, did not believe. 12 Moreover, after that, he appeared in another form to two from those walking as they were going into the country. 13 And they, going, reported it to the rest; and neither did they believe.

Mark 16:14-20

14 Novissime recumbentibus illis undecim apparuit: et exprobravit incredulitatem eorum et duritiam cordis: quia iis, qui viderant eum resurrexisse, non crediderunt.

15 Et dixit eis:

Euntes in mundum universum prædicate Evangelium omni creaturæ. 16 Qui crediderit, et baptizatus fuerit, salvus erit: qui vero non crediderit, condemnabitur. 17 Signa autem eos qui crediderint, hæc sequentur: in nomine meo dæmonia ejicient: linguis loquentur novis: 18 serpentes tollent: et si mortiferum quid biberint, non eis nocebit: super ægros manus imponent, et bene habebunt.

19 Et Dominus quidem Jesus postquam locutus est eis, assumptus est in cælum, et sedet a dextris Dei.
20 Illi autem profecti prædicaverunt ubique, Domino cooperante, et sermonem confirmante, sequentibus signis.

14 Finally, he appeared to the eleven reclining at table; and he reproached their unbelief and hardness of heart; because they did not believe those who had seen him risen again. 15 And he said to them, "Going into the whole world, preach the gospel to every creature. 16 The one who believes and is baptized will be saved; but the one who does not believe will be condemned. 17 Moreover, these signs will follow those who believe: In my name they will cast out demons; they will speak with new languages; 18 they will take up serpents; and if they drink any deadly thing, it will not hurt them; they will lay their hands upon the sick, and they will be well." 19 And the Lord Jesus indeed, after he had spoken to them, was taken up into heaven and sits at the right hand of God. 20 However, they setting out, preached everywhere, with the Lord cooperating, and confirming the word with signs that followed.

Notes

Notes

Notes

Illustrated Mark in Latin joins the growing number of Latin Resources of the LAETA Series...

Check Out These & Other Great Resources At
GlossaHouse.com

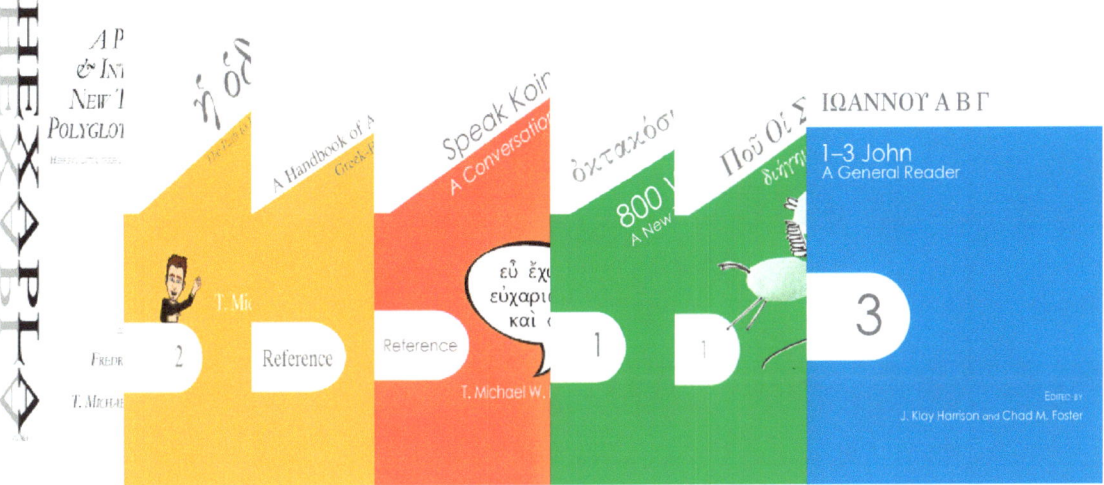

A Parallel & Interlinear New Testament Polyglot: Luke-Acts | The Path to Learning Greek | A Handbook of Ancient Greek Grammatical Terms | Speak Koine Greek | 800 Words and Images | 1-3 John: A General Reader

Learn More About The First Ever Ancient Greek Honor Society, Gamma Rho Kappa, And How You Or Your Institution Can Join Or Start A Chapter Today.

Visit GlossaHouse.com For More Details.

Learn More About The Artwork, Design, & Illustration Projects of Keith R. Neely Directly At KeithRNeely@comcast.com. Also Visit FreeIllustratedBible.com.

Look For More Volumes In The GlossaHouse Illustrated Greek-English New Testament With Illustrations By Keith R. Neely.

For More Great Resources Like This One, Visit
GlossaHouse.com

www.ingramcontent.com/pod-product-compliance
Lightning Source LLC
Chambersburg PA
CBHW041548220426
43665CB00003B/64